AUTORE

Alberto Peruffo was born in Seregno (MI) in 1968, he is a history teacher. Graduated from the University of Milan. He cooperated with the Archaeological Superintendency of Milan. He collaborates with several history magazines. He has published the following historical essays: "The Corsairs of the Kaiser" "Marvia editrice", Lombard League 1158 - 1162. The battle of Carcano, "Chillemi edizioni", The triumph of the Lombard League 1174-1176, "Chillemi edizioni", Supremacy of Rome, battles of the Cimbri and the Teutons, "Keltia editrice", Military history of the Ostrogoths, from Teodorico to Totila, "Chillemi edizioni". The Wars of the Peoples of the Sea, "Editions Arbor Sapientiae", The soldiers of the dead head division, The battle of Cortenuova, the battle of Cornate d'Adda, the battle of Capo Colonna and the battle of Desio for Soldiershop series.

PUBLISHING'S NOTES

None of unpublished images or text of our book may be reproduced in any format without the expressed written permission of Luca Cristini Editore (already Soldiershop.com) when not indicate as marked with license creative commons 3.0 or 4.0. Luca Cristini Editore has made every reasonable effort to locate, contact and acknowledge rights holders and to correctly apply terms and conditions to Content.
Every effort has been made to trace the copyright of all the photographs. If there are unintentional omissions, please contact the publisher in writing at: info@soldiershop.com, who will correct all subsequent editions.
Our trademark: Luca Cristini Editore©, and the names of our series & brand: Soldiershop, Witness to war, Museum book, Bookmoon, Soldiers&Weapons, Battlefield, War in colour, Historical Biographies, Darwin's view, Fabula, Altrastoria, Italia Storica Ebook, Witness To History, Soldiers, Weapons & Uniforms, Storia etc. are herein © by Luca Cristini Editore.

LICENSES COMMONS

This book may utilize part of material marked with license creative commons 3.0 or 4.0 (CC BY 4.0), (CC BY-ND 4.0), (CC BY-SA 4.0) or (CC0 1.0). We give appropriate attribution credit and indicate if change were made in the acknowledgments field. Our WTW books series utilize only fonts licensed under the SIL Open Font License or other free use license.

For a complete list of Soldiershop titles please contact Luca Cristini Editore on our website: www.soldiershop.com or www.cristinieditore.com. E-mail: info@soldiershop.com

Title: **THE SS CAVALRY DIVISIONS** Code.: **WTW-043 EN** by Alberto Peruffo
ISBN code: 978-88-93279666 first edition: April 2023
Language: English. Size: 177,8x254mm Cover & Art Design: Luca S. Cristini

WITNESS TO WAR (SOLDIERSHOP) is a trademark of Luca Cristini Editore, via Orio, 35/4 - 24050 Zanica (BG) ITALY.

WITNESS TO WAR

THE SS CAVALRY DIVISIONS

PHOTOS & IMAGES FROM WORLD WARTIME ARCHIVES

ALBERTO PERUFFO

BOOKS TO COLLECT

CONTENTS

Introduction..pag. 5
The beginnings of the SS cavalry...pag. 6
Operation Barbarossa..pag. 11
The fighting in the winter of 1941/42..pag. 26
Florian Geyer SS Cavalry Division..pag. 29
The division's deployment in Russia during the winter of 1942/43.......pag. 35
The rear-guard fights...pag. 37
The fighting in Hungary..pag. 66
The siege of Budapest and the annihilation of the division....................pag. 69
SS-Freiwilligen-Kavallerie-Division Maria Theresia.................................pag. 71
Early deployments to the front..pag. 73
The Battle of Budapest..pag. 76
The 37th SS-Freiwilligen-Kavallerie-Division Lützow..............................pag. 79
Conclusions..pag. 82
Hierarchy and commanders of SS cavalry divisions................................pag. 89
Bibliography...pag. 98

▲ SS on horseback parade past counter-tank units. War photographer KB. Fritsch. Nara (US Gov.)

INTRODUCTION

World War I had shown how the decisive weapon of cavalry had, by then, become obsolete in the face of the new automatic weapons and trench warfare, making it totally inadequate for its age-old task of reconnaissance and breaking through the opponent's lines. On the Western Front, position warfare, prevented any use of cavalry, so much so that even its traditional use in reconnaissance was taken over by the nascent air force weapon. On other, more dynamic fronts, such as the Eastern Front, cavalry still had its own important function, abetted by the vast areas where warfare operations unfolded; from the Baltic to the Black Sea. In the Middle East, the charge of Australian light cavalry to the Turkish stronghold at Beersheba, which prevailed against Turkish entrenched defenses despite rapid-fire guns and machine guns, had great prominence. Generally speaking, the cavalries of the period, however, were used as mounted infantry that employed horses for rapid movement and then dismounted to fight.

After the end of the World War, the use of cavalry still had a fair amount of importance with the Russian-Polish War of 1920, which saw vast masses of cavalry fighting each other, as happened in the Battle of Warsaw between Russians and Poles, won by the latter.

The advent of armored vehicles, with tanks and armored cars, forced a radical rethinking of the use of cavalry, so much so that the use of cavalry in interwar armies was greatly downsized, with aircraft and armored cars extensively employed in conflicts by colonial powers around the world.

In Germany, the rearmament of the army, beginning in 1935, led to the establishment of several cavalry units, which were considered important because of their better mobility than infantry without vehicles. Poland itself at that time had several cavalry formations flanking armored units, with which they were determined to easily defeat the Germans just as had happened less than two decades earlier against the Soviets. War with Poland broke out despite Hitler's attempts to agree on a diplomatic solution to settle the Danzig Corridor situation. This is how Matteo Simonetti in his essay "Hitler and Fichte" described the situation that led to the outbreak of the conflict with Poland:

Let us look at Poland's behavior: if indeed a psychologistic approach is to be employed in the context of explanations of the countries' conduct during the 1920s, and 1930s, then this should be directed at the "madness" of the Poles who devoted themselves, deceived by the Allies, to their own destruction. An endless list of belligerent statements, threats of invasion, expressions of contempt, invasion plans, violence against German civilians, encroachments, by the Polish press and politicians, from '25 to the beginning of German penetration...[1]

During the conflict, in September 1939, the Poles, managed to exploit their cavalry, achieving several successes, although a cavalry charge against German mechanized vehicles never occurred as legend has it.

The Germans also increasingly exploited their cavalry, especially to make up for the lack of vehicles, with army units being joined by SS units that already had a history behind them.

▲ SS Florian Geyer coat of arms.

---

1 Matthew Simonetti, Hitler and Fichte, p. 221.

THE BEGINNINGS OF THE SS CAVALRY

In 1931, well before Hitler came to power, the *Allgemeine* SS (SS generals) organized within their structure a cavalry battalion, the *Berittene SS Abteilung*. The base was located in Munich.

With the seizure of power in '33, the SS further developed the cavalry weapon, more for matters of prestige than practical utility. Cavalry schools based on the model of those in the army were created. The city of Hamburg donated a farm to the SS, which was named *Remonteanstalt des SS Hauptamntes* and would provide mounts for the Waffen SS until 1945. A cavalry academy called SS *Hauptreitschule* was established in Munich. The academy was opened in July 1936 under the direction of Hermann Fegelein[2]. The latter institution was the protagonist of many sporting events of the time of which the most distinguished representative was Martin von Barnekow already a gold medalist at the 1936 Olympic Games.

At the outbreak of war in September '39 Himmler himself wanted to set up a cavalry unit subordinate to the *Totenkopf* (SS-TV), this unit, called the 1st *SS-Totenkopf-Reiterstandarte,* was located in Berlin, consisting of 250 men, divided into four squadrons, represented the embryo of the future cavalry division. Another cavalry unit, the 2nd *SS-Totenkopf-Reiterstandarte*, of the same composition as the first, was sent to Poland on Sept. 27 with police duties.

In November 1939 the two units were reunited in Polish territory under the command of SS-Brigaführer Hermann Otto Fegelein, the structure of this unit was divided as follows:

- Stab (command company)
- Health Squadron
- 12 Squadron

▲ SS cavalry officer before the World War. Notice the peculiar insignia on the lapel.

2 Hans Georg Otto Hermann Fegelein (1906 - 1945) entered the German army in 1925 and then became a policeman in 1928 and finally served in the SS from 1933. In 1944 he married Gretl Braun, sister of Hitler's wife Eva. In the same year he was promoted SS-Gruppenführer und Generalleutnant der Waffen-SS, only to be seriously wounded in the bombing of the Wolf's Lair, Hitler's bunker. He was shot for high treason in Berlin while attempting to flee the besieged city on April 28, 1945. His name remains inextricably linked to the SS cavalry.

▲ Cavalry soldier at the time of the reconstitution of the Wehrmacht.

The 12th Squadron consisted of a mounted battery.
The unit was named *SS-Totenkopf-Reiter-Standarte* consisting of about 1,500 men. Equipment was initially scarce, especially in winter clothing, despite this the cavalrymen engaged in frantic patrol and anti-guerrilla activity in Polish territory during the cold winter of 1939/40.

▲ The mounted band of the first SS cavalry formation.

Operations in occupied Poland

During the Polish campaign, the initial tasks of the cavalry units were the classic ones of protecting supplies to the fighting units, to which were added the tasks of protecting the large German population living in Polish territory, threatened by possible reprisals from the Polish population.
With the conclusion of the campaign several squadrons of the *SS-Totenkopf-Reiter-Standarte* cavalry were dispersed throughout the vast Polish territory. The activity was mainly escorting prisoners and capturing common criminals who escaped from prisons in the confusion that followed the fighting. Ultimately the main activity was to restore order following the situation of anarchy that followed the dissolution of Polish institutions.
Polish guerrilla warfare that was trying to organize itself, especially against the German occupier, was nipped in the bud with decisiveness and ruthlessness. Anyone caught with a weapon was immediately passed by the guns on the spot. The rounding up and policing activities were assisted by the units of the SD (*Sicherheitsdienst*) security and espionage service, which was responsible for many crimes against civilians during the course of the war, the 5th Squadron distinguished itself by its ferocity in these operations especially against Jews.
One of the most important anti-guerrilla operations took place in the Kamienna Forest region on April

▲ German cavalry in training between the two world wars. Note the distinctive cavalry helmet in use since the First World War.

▼ Inspection at the SS-Totenkopf-Kavallerie-Regimenter 1 and 2 engaged in Poland, departments that preceded the existence of the Florian Geyer.

1, 1940, where a group of 300 Polish soldiers, disbanded since as far back as September 1939, were surrounded by the 1st, 7th, 8th, 9th and 10th squadrons, supported by the 51st Police Battalion, the attack was supported by artillery from the 12th Squadron. The Poles attempted to break the encirclement by taking advantage of the fact that the sector occupied by the police consisted of swampy terrain. The battle lasted several hours, and the intervention of the 10th SS Squadron prevented the worst for the police battalion. Many guerrillas had managed to escape, however, and it was not until April 8 that they were finally annihilated. For this achievement, however, some civilians from nearby villages came at the expense, who, accused of harboring the guerrillas, were deported en masse.

By the summer of 1940 any danger from guerrilla activity had finally receded and the country pacified, so that there was no further hostile activity to the German occupation forces until the summer of 1944 with the Warsaw Uprising.

In May 1940, the 12 squadrons were organized into 2 regiments for a strength of 1908 men including soldiers and officers, many were *Volksdeutsche* and some were from South Tyrol who had chosen to enlist in the German units, some of the latter soldiers who had opted to serve Germany were veterans of the 1935 Ethiopian War, fought under the flags of the Royal Italian Army.

Morale was high and, at that time, the *SS-Totenkopf-Reiter-Standarte* command organized in the Polish town of Garwolin the midsummer festival, *Sommersonnwendfeir,* with riding competitions between army and SS units. These kinds of tournaments associated with festive occasions were repeated throughout the occupation of Poland.

In addition to riding competitions, the SS cavalrymen continued their normal training. Many mounts were taken from Polish farms to keep up with the increasing numbers of the regiment, which in January 1941 was named *SS-Kavallerie Regiment,* thus the cavalry unit was taken out of the *Totenkopf*'s dependencies and became an autonomous unit within the Waffen SS.

Two regiments were formed each consisting of 12 squadrons as before, plus a transmission unit detached to the 2nd *SS-Kavallerie Regiment,* while the 7th squadron of each regiment was converted into cyclists.

▲ Column of cavalrymen scouting on the Russian steppe.

OPERATION BARBAROSSA

At the beginning of the Russian campaign, the two regiments were placed under the HSSPF of the Northern Army Group sector, responsible for rear security. The mounted SS were attached to the 87th Infantry Division with SS Stumbannführer Fassbender as liaison officer.
From June 21, the two regiments, departing from East Prussia, reached the location of Baranovichi where they formed a single cavalry brigade composed as follows:

Brigade Headquarters	SS-Standartenführer (Colonel) Hermann Fegelein.
1st SS-Kavallerie Regiment	SS Stumbannführer (major) Lombard
2nd SS-Kavallerie Regiment	SS Stumbannführer (major) Schleifenbaum

A mounted battery was assigned to Brigade Headquarters along with an antiaircraft Flak battery equipped with 20 mm guns. An antitank company was created from the 7th Squadron of each regiment.
The first clashes with the Russians occurred on July 27, when, motorized divisions of the 1st Regiment (*Voraus-Abteilung*), were engaged by the German 162 Infantry Division against elements of two Soviet divisions attempting to escape from the Pripet marshes where they had been trapped by the German advance. The same division, in the following days, was used in the rounding up of straggling Russian divisions in those vast swampy areas.
On July 30 the same unit was engaged by Russian cavalry near Novo Andreyevka where they were successfully repulsed, shortly after which the cyclist battalion also had skirmishes with the same Cossacks.
Clashes with the Cossack cavalry continued until August 6 finally decreeing an SS victory over the opposing cavalry, inflicting 200 dead and 400 prisoners on the enemy against the loss of 17 dead and 36 wounded in the ranks of the *Voraus-Abteilung* of the 1st Regiment. The 36th and 37th Soviet cavalry divisions were thus annihilated.
Meanwhile, the rest of the 1st *SS-Kavallerie Regiment*, subordinate to the German 162 Infantry Division, was engaged in reconnaissance operations along the Pripet marshes, leading to the killing of 6526 guerrillas. Thus SS-Sturmbannführer Franz Magill[3] reports in his August 12 report where he described the general situation in which the SS was fighting:

> Ukrainians and Belarusians are a particularly welcoming population.... When the troop arrived, milk, eggs and all kinds of supplies were immediately distributed, and spontaneously given in aid. Although reserved and uncommunicative, Poles and Russians were exceedingly pleased to have German soldiers around them, rejoicing to see the Bolsheviks thrown out (...).
> The roads were in a terrible state of disrepair; part sand, part mud, so the supply train squadron often had to take two days to march behind the squadrons.
> Supplies: food and oats were hard to come by because of the poor state of the roads. The voluntary donation of the inhabitants sometimes made up for the lack of food. In any case we were unable to find oats for the horses. We were unable to retrieve hay, so the horses had to feed on grass....
> Status of men: the men are in excellent condition during operations. Only a small section had to be transferred to the hospital; of those, all were able to return to the rest of the troop a few days.
> Morale is very high. We have not suffered any losses.

---
3 Franz Magill (1900 - 1972) was commander of the 2nd SS-Kavallerie Regiment from February to September 1941 and then commanded the Sondercommando "Magill" between late 1942 and early 1943, belonging to the infamous "Dirlewanger."

State of the horses: the state of the horses suffered from the lack of oat supplies and the exhausting marches they had to make each day. When, for example, a 30-kilometer sector had to be pacified in one day, this meant for horses and cavalry to cover a good 60 kilometers. This explains how many horses suffered injuries and exhaustion.... Some of the horses were replaced by trading farm horses. During the long moves, we often had to dismount so that the horses could rest. The highest horse losses were in the second and fourth squadrons.

Pacification: pacification took place as follows: the units or platoon command made contact with the mayor of a particular locality asking for details about the population. The information requested concerned the number and type of inhabitants, Ukrainians, Belarusians, and so on. Even if communists were still found in the area, any plainclothes Red Army soldier or any other person involved in Bolshevik activities. Most of the time, locals who had seen gangs or other suspicious elements came forward of their own volition. If some elements were still in the area, they were captured and, after brief interrogation, were released or shot. In each case where a police contingent was not in place, an appointment was made in proportion to the number of inhabitants taking into account the population groups in the locality. In small villages, police contingents were placed under the control of the mayor. All forms of political activity were prohibited.

Jewish murderers were shot. Only a small group of manual laborers were spared, employed by the Wehrmacht in repair work. Women and children were driven to the swamps not achieving the desired effect since the swamps were not deep enough for them to be drowned.

No communists were found. Only people who had taken part in communist activities. Much information regarding the presence of gangs was exaggerated. Jokes were generally fruitless. Once, a Polish priest was shot for his pro-Polish propaganda and exhortation to resist since Poland would rise again. Leaflets or the like were thrown near Kamien Koscyrsko.

The Ukrainian clergy were very helpful by making themselves available where they were needed....[4]

During that same period, Fegelein's cavalry units, carried out extensive anti-guerrilla operations with continuous raids conducted with extreme ferocity in a war that admitted no mercy. The Russians tortured any German prisoners they managed to capture, while the Germans destroyed villages they believed to be complicit with the Russian guerrillas.

On the morning of August 15, the 3rd squadron of the 2nd *SS-Kavallerie Regiment* was ambushed by partisans in the vicinity of the town of Turov, also in the vast area of the Pripet marshes. Compared with 2 dead, 2 missing and 9 wounded, the Russians had as many as 107 casualties.

The difficulty of movement in the swampy areas for mechanized units convinced the German command to use cavalry in that large area where thousands of Russian soldiers had taken refuge finding shelter from the German advance. The SS cavalry brigade was able to move faster than the infantry and, once they came in contact with the enemy, dismounted from their horses and engaged the battle like an infantry unit.

On August 21, Operation Turov was launched by the 2nd *SS-Kavallerie Regiment* to take the town of the same name. The operation was successful and by the morning of the same day the town was already in the hands of the SS cavalry. In the clashes to take the surrounding villages, the regiment's genius platoon repelled an attack by Russian cavalry. The day ended with a total victory for the 2nd regiment, which noted the killing of 400 enemy against 4 killed and 12 wounded; the capture of only 10 prisoners provides an idea of the ruthlessness of these battles.

Things were different for the 1st *SS-Kavallerie Regiment*, which under the command of its new commander SS-Hauptsturmführer Waldemar Fegelein (not to be confused with his brother, the brigade commander)[5], on August 18 captured 34 Russian soldiers after a short engagement.

---

4 Charles Trang, La Division Floian Geyer, p. 29-31.
5 Waldemar Fegelein (1912 - 2000) was from the very beginning of his career connected with the equestrian world and the SS cavalry division, so much so that he was enrolled in veterinary school before embarking on a military career. In 1943 he was awarded the Knight's Cross, and in 1945 he became commander of the 37th SS-Freiwilligen-Kavallerie-Division

Waldemar Fegelein developed an innovative, albeit risky, tactic based on surprise, attacking partisan bands without wasting time on reconnaissance, and was able to achieve several successes against enemies caught off guard.

On the morning of the 21st of the same month the 3rd Squadron of the 1st *SS-Kavallerie Regiment* arrived at the village of Starobin, which had been occupied by the Germans earlier, the cavalrymen discovered that the mayor and some members of the German police had been killed by partisans. The Germans elected a new mayor who was killed not even two days later by some local Jews who had joined the partisans. On the 23rd day, the entire cavalry regiment, entered the village starting the reprisal against all the local male Jews, thus 23 Jews were shot.

Operations against partisans in the area continued on August 29, when, the 1st *SS-Kavallerie Regiment, under* the orders of Waldemar Fegelein attacked an island northwest of Kochos where the Russians had entrenched themselves. The direct assault on the island was successful; in a short time the SS killed 154 Russians, wounding 117, and captured 37 others who were trying to escape.

The raking operations in the marshes were halted on September 10 when the SS cavalry was ordered to blockade isolated Red Army groups trying to escape from the Kiev pocket in which they had been trapped by the German advance. The SS cavalry brigade succeeded in surrounding and annihilating a section of 500 Russian soldiers near the town of Krasnyy, capturing 38 officers and killing 384 of the enemy without casualties. For this operation Waldemar Fegelein was awarded the Iron Cross First Class. His brother Herman took stock of the operations:

> Enemy forces were always wiped out when they belonged to the regular forces of the Russian Army. The greatest difficulties were posed by the partisans. Militarily they were the greatest threat found behind a fighting army. Ruthless, brave to the point of annihilation, with Asiatic cruelty. This enemy forced our units to remain on constant alert relying on their extensive organization and excellent communication networks. Their familiarity with the terrain, their constant blocking of roads by sowing mines and destroying bridges, their ability to quickly entrench themselves in machine-gun dens at strategic points, and in their display of calm during the hardest fighting in the swamps, are the hallmarks of their fighting ability[6].

After this operation, the SS cavalry brigade returned to operate in the swampy areas of the Pripet, the units were scattered over a large area that could be covered by cavalry mobility.

On Oct. 5, the brigade was sent to operate in the Toropets sector under the 253 Infantry Division, with the task of protecting supply convoys and the railroad in the area.

Anti-partisan activity continued unabated, and numerous ambushes were foiled. In the meantime, the weather became increasingly harsh, the Russian winter was now approaching.

One of the last anti-partisan operations before the Russian offensive took place in the first week of December in the area northwest of Putiwl. Here the Russians offered some resistance thanks in part to the support of a Pzkpfw III tank captured from the Germans some time earlier. The SS eventually prevailed at the cost of 3 killed and 8 wounded against the killing of 73 partisans and the capture of 93 prisoners. Over the next few days the SS cavalry were involved in a series of minor skirmishes that caused numerous losses to the Soviets confirming the SS cavalry brigade as one of the best German units in the ruthless anti-guerrilla warfare.

"Lützow" and then returned to his previous post with the SS-FHA. After his imprisonment in an American camp he ran a riding stable.
6 Ibid, p. 35.

▲ Florian Geyer cavalry in Russia.

▼► Sequence of images of the faces of Florian Geyer soldiers engaged in MG machine gun exercises taken by war reporter Fritsch.

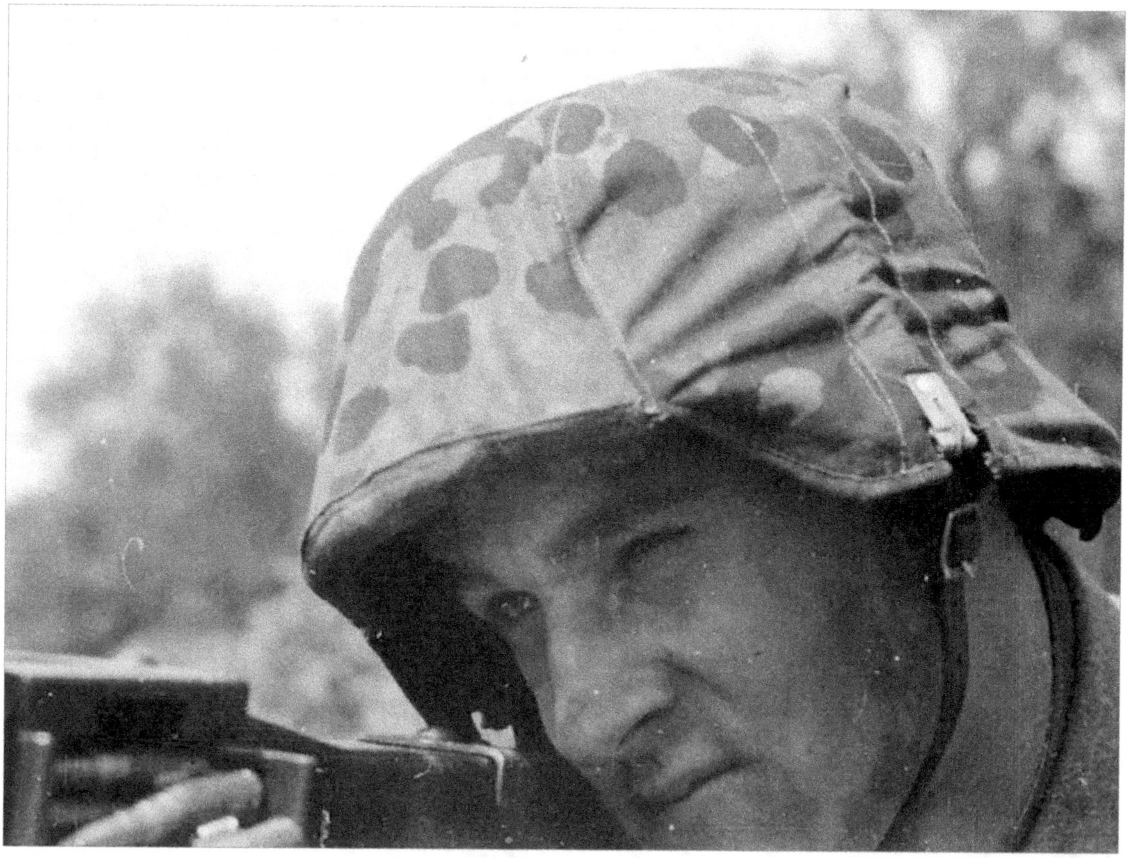

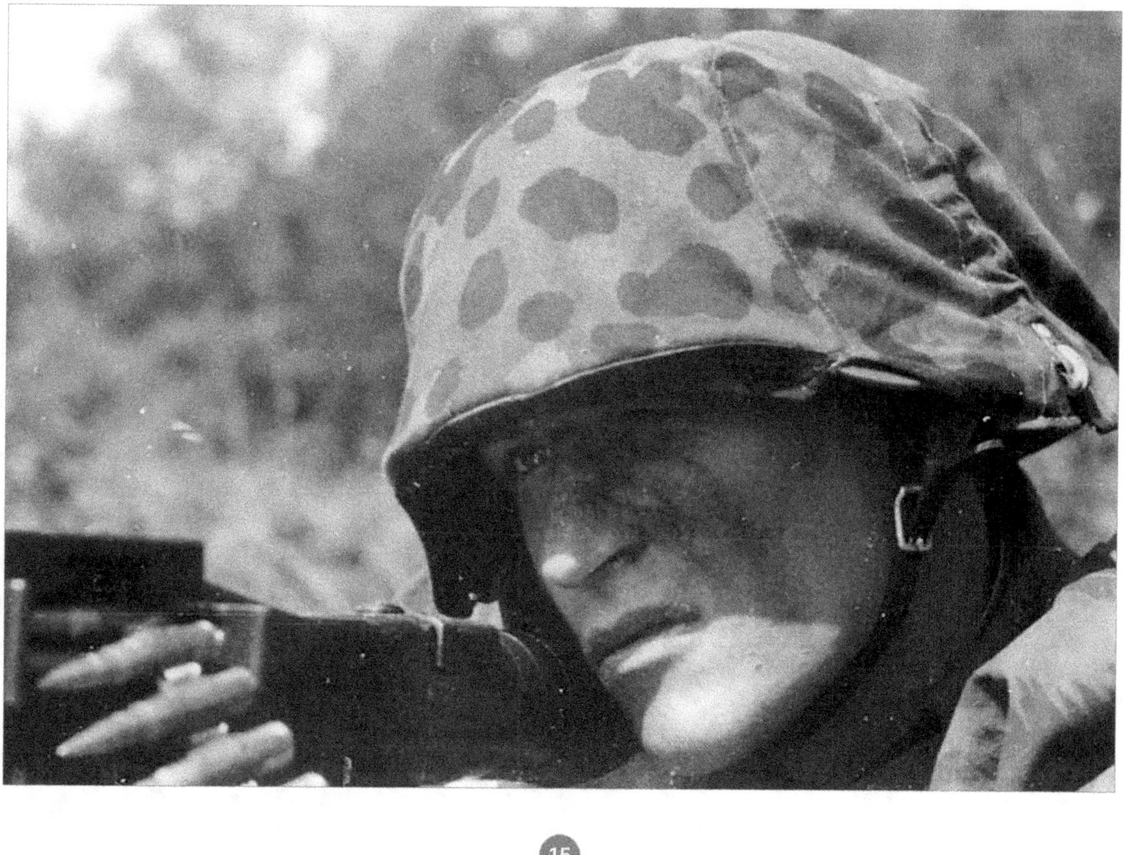

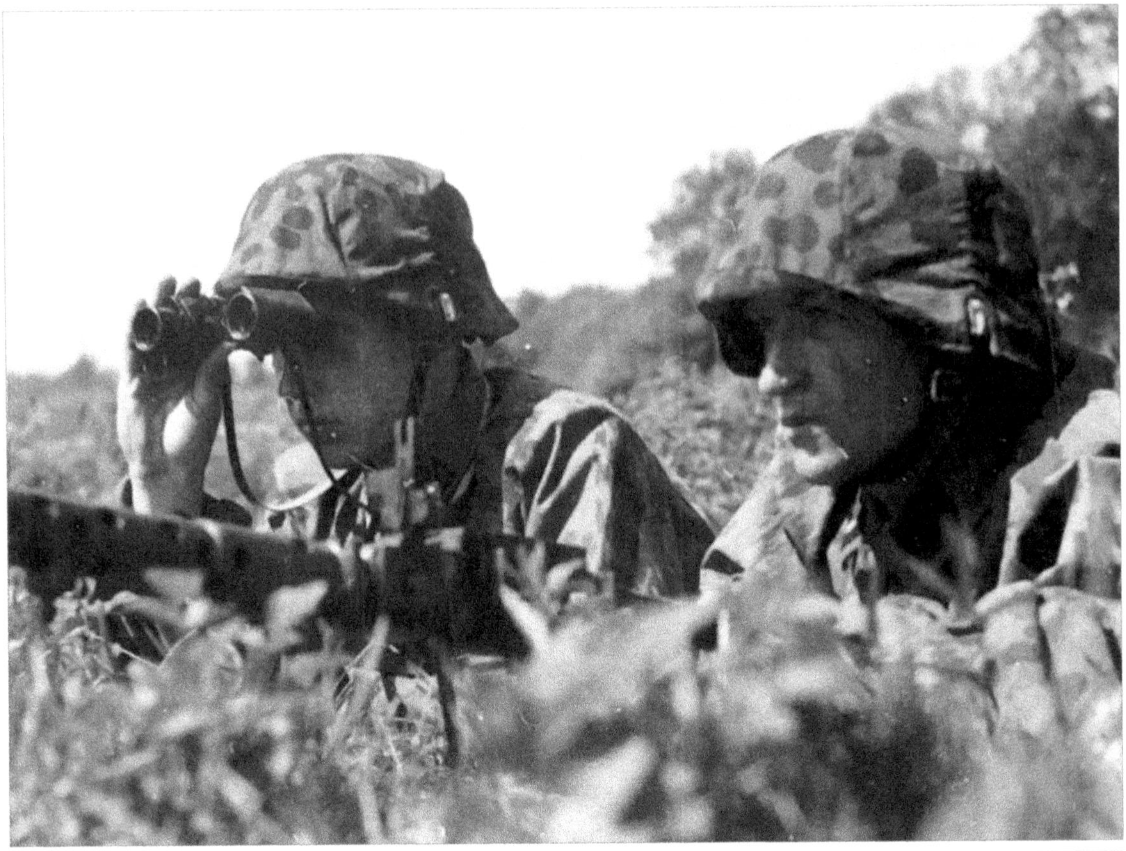

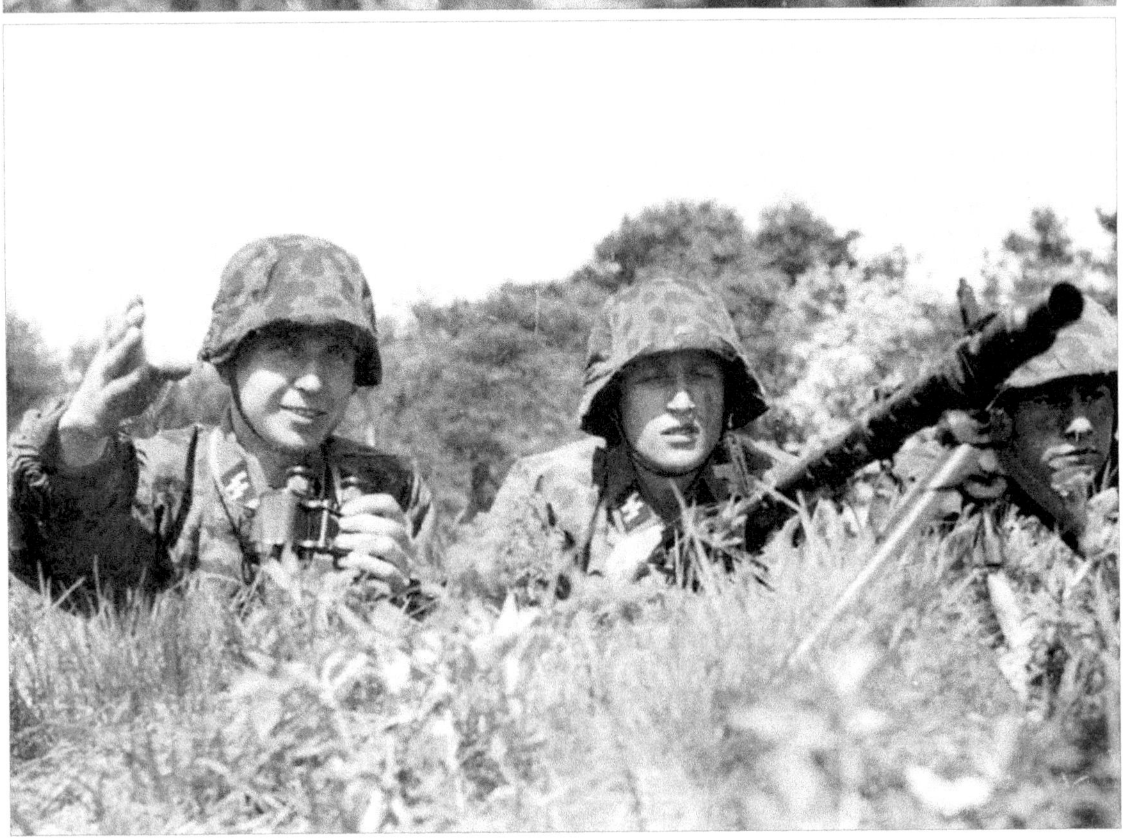

▲ Cavalry platoon in the brushwood, scouting.

▲ Florian Geyer cavalry marching across the Russian steppe. Photo by F. Fritsch (Nara US Gov.)

▼ Men of the Florian Geyer division next to the camouflaged vehicles of the department. Photo by K. Hoppe (Nara US Gov.)

▲ ▼ Cavalry units of the Florian Geyer taken by the camera of F. Fritsch, a well-known photoreprter of the period (Nara US Gov.)

▲ SS soldier engaged in anti-guerrilla operations in the rear of the Russian front.

▲ A moment's pause for a cavalryman.

▲ River ford.

▲ Florian Geyer officer in a moment of combat in Russia.

▲ SS Florian Geyer NCO in snow camouflage outfit engaged in action.

▲ The fatigue of fighting along the steppes and in the Russian marshes are clearly evident in this image.

THE FIGHTING IN THE WINTER OF 1941/42

From December, the cavalry brigade was deployed for security duties along the Weliki-Luki railway line vital for 9th Army supplies. Meanwhile, the offensive on Moscow had stalled on December 5, and the next day the massive Soviet counteroffensive was triggered, threatening to overwhelm the entire Central Army Group.

On Dec. 23, the cavalry brigade was placed on alert, ready for action on the front lines. In early 1942, the cavalry brigade was placed under direct army command for the first time within the 23rd Army Corps.

On January 2, Hitler, forbade the 9th Army any further retreat, ordering it to hold out to the bitter end in prohibitive environmental conditions. The snow and cold were such that for movement the cavalry brigade built sleds to be pulled by their own horses.

The Soviet 34th Army had crossed the Volga on January 4, opening a 15-kilometer gap between the 256th and 206th German infantry divisions. The SS cavalry brigade was ordered to close the breach in the Rshew sector, reporting to the 206th Infantry Division. Although supported by *Kamfgruppe* Kaestner with 300 infantrymen and an artillery regiment, the Germans had to yield to enemy pressure by slowly withdrawing on Jan. 9. The Russians' attempt to encircle the 23rd Army Corps from the north interrupted the pressure in the sector held by the SS.

While the rest of the brigade fought alongside the 206th Infantry Division the cyclist battalion was further north protecting the left flank of the 253rd Infantry Division in the Pyeno sector. On Jan. 9, the battalion was attacked by two Soviet divisions forcing the Germans to abandon the town of Pyeno, but a counterattack was launched that night that allowed the SS to recapture the town, which was again lost two days later. These battles cost the cyclist battalion 75 percent of their original strength.

On January 18, the Soviets again attempted to separate the 23rd Army Corps from the 6th Army Corps, which was located to the south. The SS returned to the fight with a counterattack to retake the villages Kharino and Shapalevo that had fallen into enemy hands. After hours of hard fighting the two villages were recaptured and the Russians pushed back.

On the 22nd, the new 9th Army commander, General Model, launched a general counterattack using the 1st Armored Division as the lead unit.

The SS cavalry were to depart from the newly recaptured village of Olenino with the support of a battalion of StuG tank fighters; their main purpose was to protect the right flank of the 206th Infantry Division. The attack was a success, not only foiling any threat of encirclement by the 23rd Army Corps, but also leading to the isolation of two Soviet armies the 29th and 39th with elements of the 11th Cavalry Corps.

The Russians in an attempt to escape encirclement attacked the 206th Infantry Division from behind. Once again the SS cavalry was employed, which succeeded in blocking the Russians tightened by now in a large pocket. The casualties in the course of these battles numbered over 370, many more, however, were cases of frostbite, the better the condition of the mounts allowed the brigade an unchanged degree of mobility.

On February 4, the villages of Tarasovo, Upyri and Pogorelki were captured in violent house-to-house fighting. The next day the brigade became part of *Kamfgruppe* Raesfeld, which held the southernmost side of that sector of the front.

In the following days the SS captured other villages fighting in temperatures of -40 C°. At Chertolino, German cavalrymen killed 200 enemies while capturing 100, receiving compliments from the commander of the 23rd Army Corps, General Schubert.

On the morning of Feb. 7 the cavalry brigade joined units of the German 1st Armored Division near the village of Chertolino. The Soviets to prevent this connection immediately counterattacked, recapturing the village.

The following day the SS was placed in charge of the 1st *Panzerdivision*; in the fighting that followed the Germans managed to restore the situation in their favor. Distinguished in these battles was SS-Obersturmführer Rudolf Maeker, who, on his own initiative, launched a lightning attack to the northeast of the sector involved in the offensive, capturing the village of Siwino.

The final offensive against the Soviet pocket was triggered on February 10, the SS cavalrymen's main task being to round up the isolated Russian units inside the pocket. Fighting took place in the cold forests of those areas, often hand-to-hand, as happened, on February 15, to Maeker who, with his squadron reduced to only 30 men, managed to destroy 9 bunkers in close combat, thus succeeding in protecting the right flank of the cavalry brigade. This is how the action is remembered in the divisional diary:

> On February 21, 1942, assault on Mantrovkie: in an attempt to attack the village area by the 1st and 2nd SS-Kavallerie Regiment along fairly extensive terrain, SS-Obersturmführer Rudolf Maeker led the attack in a way that the enemy thought of a full-scale German offensive. Thanks to this diversion, carried with considerable courage, the charge of the rest of the brigade was crowned with success[7].

On the 18th of the same month, the annihilation battle could be said to have ended with the total German victory and the loss for the Russians of two armies.

From February 22 to 23, the Russians launched a series of local night counteroffensives in an attempt to recapture some villages including Olenino. They were all repulsed by the SS, which caused heavy losses to the enemy, this despite the numerical inferiority of the Germans.

The first weeks of March saw the Russians retreating to a new defensive line further east and the Germans in pursuit.

On March 6, the SS captured the village of Shitiki, killing 350 enemy soldiers in house-to-house fighting. The next day the offensive resumed northward along with the 1st *Panzerdivision*, this allowed them to surround other Russian divisions that were annihilated in the following days.

For the valor demonstrated by his brigade during the winter campaign, SS-Standartenführer Hermann Fegelein was awarded the Knight's Cross and recalled home, and in his place in command of the brigade was placed SS Stumbannführer Gustav Lombard[8] already in command of the 1st SS-Kavallerie Regiment at the beginning of the Russian campaign.

The brigade had lost 2100 men dead and wounded out of a total of 3100 men who had served the brigade since the summer of 1941, now all that remained was a single regiment. Because of these losses the unit was withdrawn from the Russian front in April to be reconstituted as a fighting force at Debica in Poland. Only *Kampfgruppe* Zehender remained at the front, which, reporting to the 1st Armored Division, continued in roundup operations until mid-May when it too was withdrawn to Debica for a rest period.

---

7 Ibid, p. 47.
8 Gustav Lombard (1895 - 1992) had joined the SS in 1933 by joining the cavalry stationed in Berlin, the 7th SS-Reiterstandart. With the rank of Hauptsturmführer he joined the Waffen-SS of the Totenkopf cavalry regiment where he spent the first years of the war passing into the Florian Geyer. For a short time, from October 28, 1943, he commanded the 29th Waffen-Grenadier-Division der SS in Italy as SS-Standartenführer and then took command of the Florian Geyer before moving on to command the Northern Division and then the 31st SS-Freiwilligen-Grenadier-Division and ending up captured by the Soviets ending the war in their captivity with the rank of Brigadeführer und Generalmajor der Waffen-SS, being released only in 1955.

▲ Hermann Fegelein with his officers.
▼ SS cavalrymen in action during the winter from a shot by the war reporter Buschulte.

FLORIAN GEYER SS CAVALRY DIVISION

It was during the period of reorganization at Debica in Poland that, on June 1, 1942, Hitler gave orders to transform the cavalry brigade into a division, increasing its staffing.

The new division was named *SS-Kavallerie Division* and consisted of three cavalry regiments each consisting of six squadrons plus a motorized reconnaissance battalion, a transmission battalion, an engineer battalion, an antitank battalion, and an antiaircraft battery. An artillery regiment consisting of three battalions completed the staffing of the new division. An assault tank battery and an antitank company were also included on September 28.

The recruits were mostly young *Volksdeutsche* (as many as 80 percent of the headcount); veterans completed the cadres of the new departments.

Equipment and material was greatly improved, obsolete French or Czechoslovakian armaments were withdrawn and replaced with German ones.

Command of the division was given to SS-Brigadeführer Wilhelm Bittrich, who replaced Fegelein commanded at Hitler's headquarters.

The division was declared ready for combat by mid-August, but for Bittrich his recruits were not yet ready, he asked, thus, Himmler to postpone the division's deployment to the front.

The SS commander granted Bittrich's requests in part by allowing him to continue training for most of his men; however, he asked that two *Kampfgruppe* be created with the best-trained units to be deployed on the Russian front.

The two units were composed as follows:

Kampfgruppe Z - Obersturmbannführer Zehender
2nd Cavalry Regiment
1st battalion of the artillery regiment
reconnaissance battalion

Kampfgruppe L - Sturmbannführer Lombard
1st Cavalry Regiment
veterinary company

In September the *Kampfgruppe* were sent to the Velikije Luki and Velish sector in the north central part of the Russian front. The SS were attached to the 330th Infantry Division and immediately employed in anti-partisan operations in the forests and swamps of the area. In those northern regions, the autumn weather, came very quickly with persistent rains that made the ground a sea of mud that made movement difficult for the vehicles, slowing them down to a standstill. Only the cavalry division remained one of the few units still with a fair amount of mobility, so much so that, the Germanic command, thought of employing it in the front line rather than in anti-guerrilla actions behind the front lines, showing how, the employment of horses, was still important in certain environmental conditions.

On September 20, the Germans launched a local offensive that saw the 330th Division engaged with the SS in repelling an attack by young Soviet infantrymen from Central Asia in the Lake Saposho sector. In recapturing some villages on September 26, the SS suffered heavy losses. On October 3, the town of Vlashkina was captured by *Kampfgruppe* Z thanks to a diversionary action by the 1st Cavalry Regiment.

The onset of autumn with its rains blocked the mechanized vehicles, halting all offensive action. Only the cavalry forces were still able to move over the swampy terrain.

In those days the front was stabilized and the SS was brought to the rear where the anti-aircraft battalion joined.

In mid-October the 2nd regiment was employed in anti-partisan operations between Burdukova and Demidov, while the rest of the division reached the front under the 6th Army Corps.

Subsequently, beginning on Nov. 9, the 1st Regiment's squadrons were deployed in combing operations in the Vodnevka area, where the 1st Squadron was heavily engaged in close clashes with partisans in Simonovka where, in a few minutes of firefighting, it had 27 men killed and 35 wounded.

The November snowfalls suggested the creation of a ski unit within the cavalry division, so a ski battalion was formed at Potepovo, 628 soldiers strong, 90 non-commissioned officers and 16 officers, divided into 4 infantry companies plus a battery and an engineer platoon, most of the soldiers came from the reconnaissance battalion.

Immediately this unit was deployed to the rear for anti-guerrilla operations.

▲ An image of the two Fegelein brothers photographed by the war reporter Hoppe.

▼ Himmler reviews the SS cavalry at the front in May 1942.

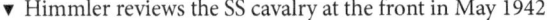

▲ Una curiosa foto rubata di Hans Georg Otto Hermann Fegelein, mitico generale tedesco delle Waffen-SS.

▲ Cavalry division commander Hermann Fegelein engaged in the field.

▲ Fegelein, in the centre, with Gustav Lombard to his left.

▼ Study of a map in the area of operation.

▲ Funeral service for a division officer killed in action.

▼ SS war cemetery.

THE DIVISION'S DEPLOYMENT IN RUSSIA DURING THE WINTER OF 1942/43

The month of November saw the alternation of division command between Obersturmbannführer Lombard and Bittrich for a short time.

At the end of November the Russian winter offensive was triggered that would lead to the German defeat at Stalingrad on the southern front, but, in the north central sector, things went differently. The Russians attacked west of Rzhev on November 25, involving Army Group Center. The SS Cavalry Division's task was initially to cover a 20-kilometer gap between the *Luftwaffe*'s 2nd Field Division and the 197th Infantry Division. On November 28, the 1st and 2nd cavalry regiments launched a counterattack to relieve the SS's bordering positions. The next day the battle reached a critical point when the Russians attacked the division's right flank in the Pokrovskiy Forest area where a fierce battle was ignited with many losses on both sides, but which eventually saw the Russians pushed back.

On December 9, the Germans went on the offensive in that sector of the front, attempting a pincer maneuver with three divisions to the north: the 20th Motorized, the 19th *Panzerdivision and the* SS cavalry, and from the south with the 1st *Panzerdivision* and the *Grossdeutschland* regiment. In the clashes that followed, the 1st Cavalry Regiment, had to fight against the entire 17th Soviet Guard Division. Despite being outnumbered, the Germans managed to corral two mechanized brigades, the 17th Guard Division itself plus elements from three other brigades, into the pocket, known as Beliye. In the five days of fighting that followed, only a few Russians managed to break free from the grip that held them. The German victory was complete and the northern front was stabilized. The SS had many losses during this action. The skier battalion suffered most, which was disbanded and its men returned to the reconnaissance battalion.

Cavalrymen had to contend with a lack of experience in front-line combat, especially officers who often put entire units at risk.

As of Dec. 31, however, the division had a staff of 310 officers and 10569 soldiers and non-commissioned officers.

The early days of 1943 saw the division deployed in its more appropriate role of anti-guerrilla warfare. Placed in the rear of Beliye in the Nikitinka area with the task of patrolling vast areas of ice-covered, partisan-infested forests and swamps. At that time a series of offensives were launched to capture some villages, which were sometimes recaptured by the Russians during the following night. In February, Operation Sternlauf resulted in the capture of 1067 prisoners and the death of 1882 partisans who were killed during the operation.

SS-Unterscharführer Albert Schwenn of the 5th Squadron of the First SS Regiment recounted his experience in those actions:

> In 1940, I volunteered for the Waffen SS and appeared before the medical board. Of about 50 men, only eight were selected. None of the others proved to have the right qualifications. This would change later when the 1.60 m tall *Volkdeutschland* comrades were recruited! When I finally got the long-awaited call, I was very disappointed at first. I joined the cavalry, when I would have liked to join the armored or motorcycle units. But my father was as pleased as I was sorry; he liked horses more than anything else, and he had no idea what the difference might be between mounting military and civilian horses. So, in October 1942, I became an SS-Reiter (...). The training was not exactly what sturdy young comrades needed in raising their enthusiasm to become soldiers. Throughout the whole period of training, from beginning to end, we went hungry with some turnips from the warehouses consumed raw.

At the beginning of February 1943, we were transferred to the front. And in the following days, we were employed in hunting partisans, although few of us in the 5th Squadron of the 1st *SS-Reiter Regiment* had ever seen one. We fired only once, from a village three kilometers away where we had made a brief stop at the edge of a forest. For two months we lived in an old Russian cavalry barracks in La pichi, near Ossifichi. When we were off again, up at 4:00 a.m. and on horseback at 5:00. We dismounted before we had covered 5 kilometers so as to slow the horses' pace. Around 9:00 we were overtaken by a column of motorized vehicles that had left after us. The comrades were sitting quietly leaning next to each other in their Kafka.15s (troop transport vehicle), dozing. Some military genius had us take up position one night on a hillside, inviting Ivan (the Russians) to practice shooting at us the next morning. Before long I remained the only gunner with gunners 2, 3 and 4 all killed. Our regimental commander came to the front line in his command vehicle and left me there. For three days we remained fixed with the enemy's eyes on us, ending up shot, thus ending my service in the SS cavalry division[9].

▲ SS subsistence wagon.

▼ Officers' canteen of the SS Cavalry Division.

---

9 Ibid, p. 91.

THE REAR-GUARD FIGHTS

On February 15, division commander Bittrich was assigned to command the new SS Hohenstaufen division and was replaced for a time by SS - standartenführer Freitag until April when Hermann Fegelein returned in his place.

A new Russian offensive on Feb. 12 required SS cavalrymen to intervene on the Briansk front line, threatening the central sector of the German defensive line.

Not all of the cavalry division was sent to the line, however, but Obersturmbannführer Zehender's *Kampfgruppe Z* was reorganized, consisting mainly of the 2nd Cavalry Regiment.

This unit, placed 30 km south of Dmitrovsk, launched a series of counterattacks beginning in March against the flanks of enemy forces, preventing the Soviets from encircling German forces in that sector.

In April *Kampfgruppe* Z also returned to the rest of the division deployed in the rear.

In May, the SS cavalry division, participated with some police battalions in anti-partisan operations in the area of the Pripet marshes and the nearby Dnieper River. The Russian forces were numerous and well organized, even equipped with German *Luftwaffe* uniforms. On May 12, the reconnaissance battalion alone faced over 600 partisans, capturing about 500 vehicles of all kinds hidden in the forest. But, as was often the case in the fight against partisans, the bulk of the enemy forces dispersed into small groups and slipped past the German raking lines, putting themselves in harm's way.

The environmental conditions in the swamps were sometimes even worse than the enemies, having to contend with mosquitoes, insects, humidity and mud that made all movement difficult.

Antiguerrilla operations continued, however, until late June when, on July 19, SS cavalry surrounded a large group of partisans and, in the following battle, with the loss 22 killed and 56 wounded, boasted 1256 enemy killed, many of them shot, with 206 Ukrainian prisoners. Ludwig Mückl witnessed the difficult environment where these battles occurred:

> We left Karachev for Gomel, passing through Briansk. We reached a boundless forest at Rechitsa on the Dnieper. Our action in the swamps was made much more difficult by the constant rains and the unbearable torment caused by mosquitoes. Smoking kept them away momentarily, but not for long especially since I was not a smoker. We were provided with a mosquito net that we could put on our helmets. However, the mosquito net was not of much help since the beasts came through even the smallest holes. It was tremendous. In the "wet triangle" our division served at Rechitsa. This was reported directly to the *Führer*'s command at the Eagle's Nest in East Prussia. We then had to go back to the swamps of Pripet and I was ordered to build a base along a road in the forest. After this I was commanded to escort ten men. We lived well, every day going to nearby villages to get some eggs. After not long we became so insolent that we would fire three shots in the air before entering the village so that we would collect eggs only by passing by the houses. Later in the evening, there was always a big party....[10]

Following the Battle of Kursk, the Soviets launched a violent offensive along the entire front line beginning in August '43.

The cavalry division was transported by rail to the Donetz Basin where it arrived on August 21, in the sector south of Merefa where it was assigned 8 km of front.

On August 26, the Russians attacked the SS positions with numerous tanks that clashed with StuG IIIs of the assault tank battery and Marder IIs of the anti-tank battalion. With difficulty they were repulsed. The next day, the Russian tanks, returned to the attack, managing to surround many units of the division that were only liberated by the Germans with the use of all available reserves of the division. After 8 days of continuous attacks along the entire front line, the Germans began to retreat, however, engaging the Russians in a series of violent rear-guard battles.

---

10 Ibid, p. 97.

Particularly distinguished in this phase was the 4th Squadron of the 1st Regiment, which, under the command of Obersturmführer Johannes Göhler, managed to block an attack of 33 tanks for an entire day, destroying as many as 15 of them in close combat, often using Teller mines. Also the next day, Göhler, managed to stop an entire Russian regiment with the support of two assault guns, this in spite of the fact that already from the early morning hours, he and his men had been subjected to heavy bombardment from both artillery and the enemy air force. Göhler for this action was decorated with the Knight's Cross and the German Gold Cross,

On Sept. 17, in the course of these violent rearguard battles, Oberscharführer Alfred Nowak was also awarded the Knight's Cross, when in command of the 3rd Squadron, also of the 1st Regiment, he led, with a handful of men, a series of counterattacks against the opposing positions, but was killed in the fighting.

In those days the division commander Fegelein was wounded in the arm and was replaced by Obersturmbannführer Streckenbach.

In mid-September, the cavalry division was involved in a series of tough clashes at Kitay-Gorod.

On October 22 the cavalry division was renamed the 8th *Kavallerie Division* and the 1st, 2nd and 3rd regiments were renumbered 15th, 16th and 17th respectively while, another cavalry regiment, the 18th was in formation. All other units in the division were given the number 8. The organization chart of the new division in the fall of 1943 was as follows:

- Divisionsstab (Division Command)
- SS Kav regt 15 (formerly regt 1)
- SS Kav regt 16 (formerly regt 2)
- SS Kav regt 17 (formerly regt 3)
- SS Kav regt 18 (formerly regt 4)
- SS Panzerjäger Abteilung 8
- SS Sturmgeschütz (StuG III assault tanks) Abteilung 8
- SS Artillerie regt (motorized) 8
- SS Flak Abteilung 8
- SS Nachrichten Abteilung (motorized) 8
- SS (Panzer) Aufklärungs Abteilung 8
- SS Radfahr Aufklärungs Abteilung 8
- SS Pioneer Batallion (motorized) 8

Meanwhile, the division, had reached the defense lines of the important town of Krivoy Rog, on the southern front in Ukraine, where it had to sustain a series of heavy fighting against an enemy now superior in every field.

On Nov. 21, the SS, entrenched in snow, had to endure a violent Soviet offensive, with squadrons down to a strength of about 20 men, often commanded by non-commissioned officers. On the 27th of the same month, the Russians broke through on the division's right flank, taking advantage of the rugged terrain there. Only thanks to the intervention of the artillery regiment was it possible to close the dangerous gap in the German deployment.

On December 6, the division's survivors were given orders to launch a counteroffensive toward the town of Tovarka, which they managed to occupy only to lose it the next day.

Over the next few weeks most of the division was placed, first, in reserve and, then, transferred to Croatia for a period of rest and reorganization.

Only a *Kampfgruppe* formed by the 15th Cavalry Regiment and the 1st Battery of the 8th Artillery Regiment remained along the front line aggregated with the 6th *Panzerdivision* north of Kirovograd where, during a counterattack, it managed to capture a large amount of supplies assigned to the Red Army.

At the end of December the *Kampfgruppe* was assigned to the 389th Infantry Division with which it continued to operate along the Tolepino - Kamenka line; it was in that sector that the Russians managed to break through the lines held by the cavalry on January 10, 1944, forcing them to retreat to Kirovograd. The latter town soon found itself surrounded by Russian troops, forcing the surviving German forces to abandon the town at a bare brisk pace on the night of Jan. 9-10, scattering into small groups and abandoning their heavy armament.

Once the sun rose, the SS, reorganizing in the town of Andreyevka, faced a violent attack by Russian infantry that was repulsed only after violent close combat.

On Jan. 20, the survivors of the *Kampfgruppe*, were finally withdrawn from the front and sent to Croatia where they joined the rest of the division, which, together with the new regiment, numbered 5182 officers and soldiers.

Another unit of the Cavalry Division had remained in Russia, this one was the 17th Cavalry Regiment, which, after a brief stint in the rear, was sent to the front in the Brest-Litovsk sector in early 1944. During the first clashes in late January the regimental commander Obersturmbannführer Zehender was wounded, and replaced by Sturmbannführer Janssen who led his men in retaking the town of Rossysze on February 9. On the 27th of the same month, the Soviets launched an offensive that forced the SS into the defensive in the sector northeast of the town of Kovel. The battle was very bloody and Janssen himself fell in the fighting, later replaced by Hauptsturmführer Schiefer.

On March 16, SS-Gruppenführer Gille, who had just emerged from the bloody Cherkassy pocket in order to better coordinate relief efforts, arrived at the town of Kovel. A few days later Kovel, with the 17th regiment inside, was surrounded by the Russians, soon reduced to a few hundred men led by SS-Hauptsturmführer Ameiser. This is how a cadet officer of the regiment described these ruthless battles:

> After leaving Riga for Poznan (Posen), I joined the RAD (labor service) in Magdeburg in 1942. In 1943 I joined the Waffen SS as a volunteer on the condition that I could serve in the cavalry. My reasons for this were due to a certain idea I had of the elite, encouraged by the motto "Comradeship and Quality," also a chat with my father, who had been a knight of the Czar and told me, "Join the cavalry, it is bearable to be a cavalryman." So in the summer of 1943, in Schiratz, near Litzmannstadt, I joined the 3rd regiment of the SS cavalry division. Until the new year, we were in the training camp, receiving mainly infantry instruction and riding mediocre horses. In January 1944 I had to be hospitalized, thus not being able to leave with my regiment for Kovel. Later, together with 30 or 40 other comrades, we formed the *Regimentsnachkommando* with which we had to carry materials, weapons and supplies. The regiment was dismounted and used as a type of "corps," which was widespread in isolated units consisting of engineers or railroad employees. Since all officers and commanders had been killed, my squadron was commanded by an SS-Unterscharführer. The commander of my squadron, Willi Geier, was engaged in another sector of the front (from the strength of a battalion). I was promoted to SS-Sturmann at Kovel, obtaining the assault insignia and bronze decoration for close combat. To these was added, as squad commander, the Iron Cross second class for fighting southwest of Kovel. Our unit had to move along the western banks of the Turija taking up positions around Kolkhoze. During that same night we were attacked by preponderant Soviet forces and forced to retreat. The western bank was very steep while the eastern bank was flat. I covered the isolated squads and platoons as they retreated, otherwise they would have been an easy target. I was the last of my squad to leave the west bank. During the night of Easter Saturday, just before the encirclement was broken by SS-Division "Wiking," I was wounded by a bullet through my forearm...[11]

Only on the morning of March 30 did German units, and, among the first, the 9th SS *Panzergrenadier* "Germania" regiment belonging to Wiking, succeed in breaking the encirclement, freeing the city from the siege. The 17th regiment remained on the line until April in that sector, fighting on terrain made impassable to vehicles by mud caused by torrential rains. Later the cavalrymen were sent to Hungary where they would go on to form the nucleus of the new cavalry division: the 22nd *SS Freiwilligen Kavallerie* Division, the future Maria Theresia Division.

---

11 Ibid, p. 143.

▲ Ukraine 1943. SS-Sturmbannführer Walter Drexler (8th SS-Cavalry Division Florian Geyer) and SS-Obersturmbannführer Otto Weidinger (2nd SS-Panzer-Division Das Reich) together on the battlefield.

▲ The following photographs (p. 41 to p. 46) depict a razing of a Russian village as part of an anti-guerrilla operation.

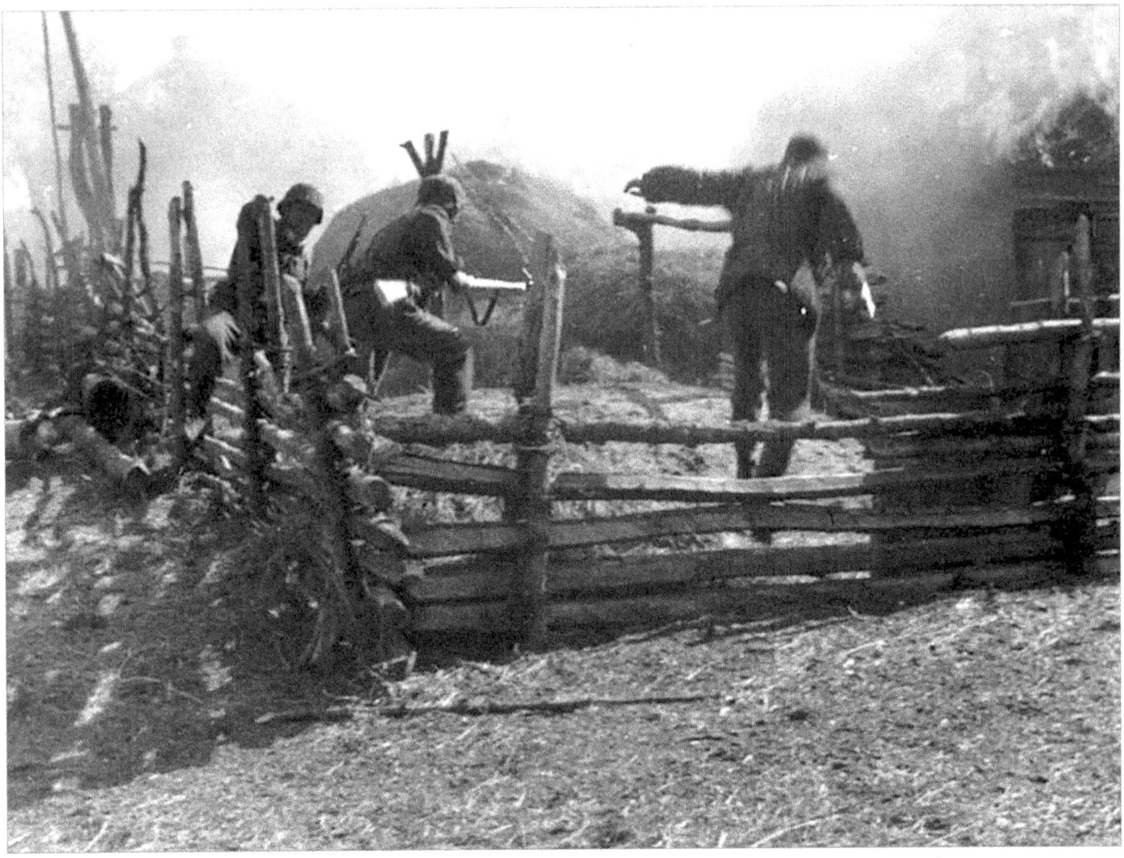

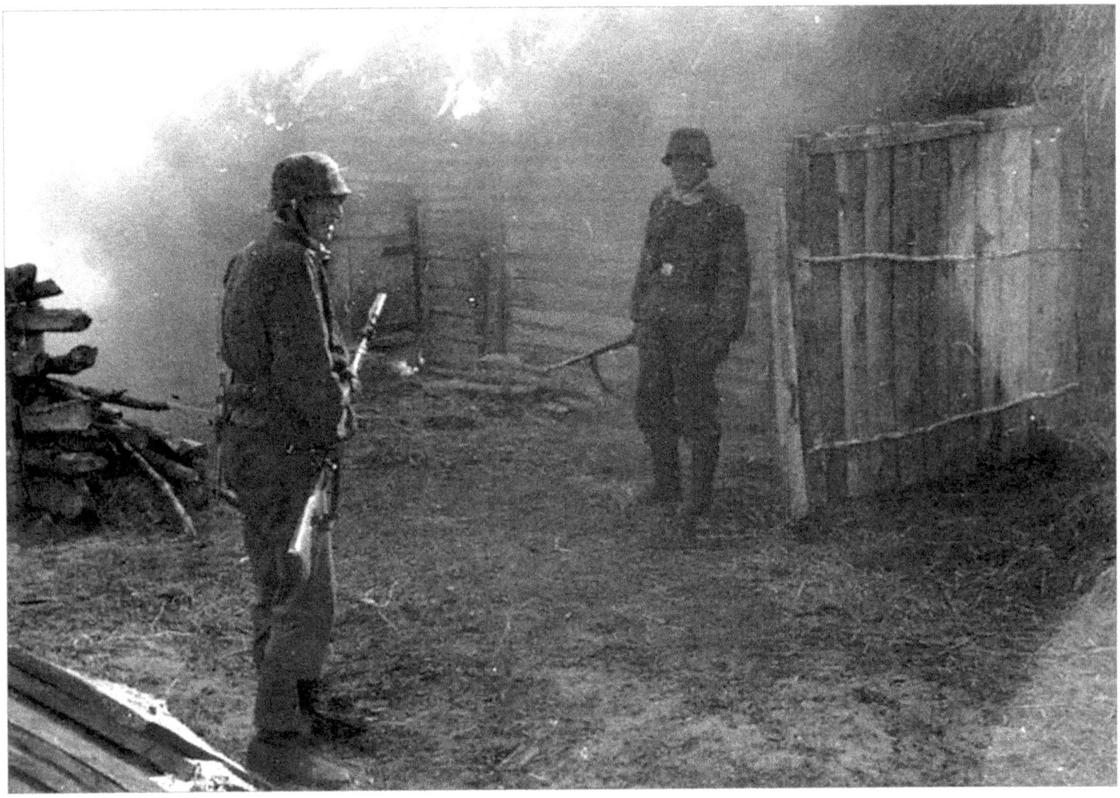

▲ SS of the Florian Geyer motorbike department in action.

▲ Anti-guerrilla fighting.

▼ Motorbike department.

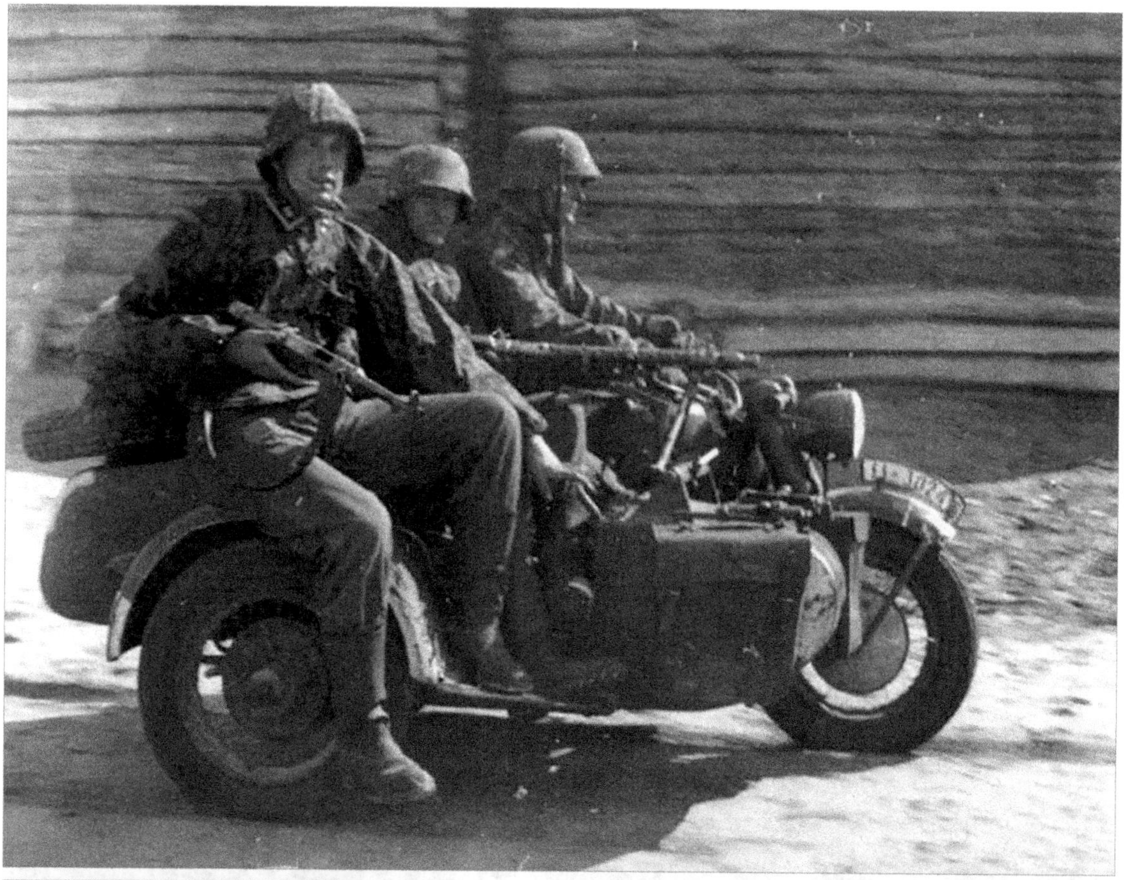

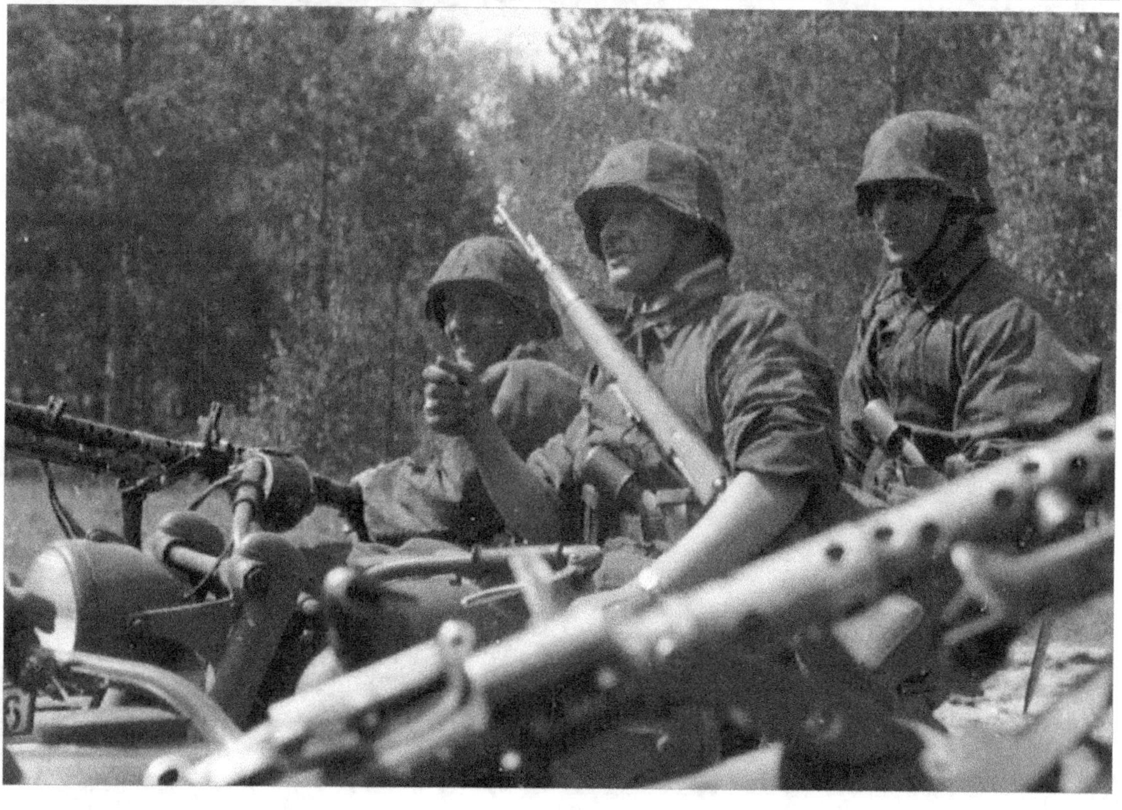

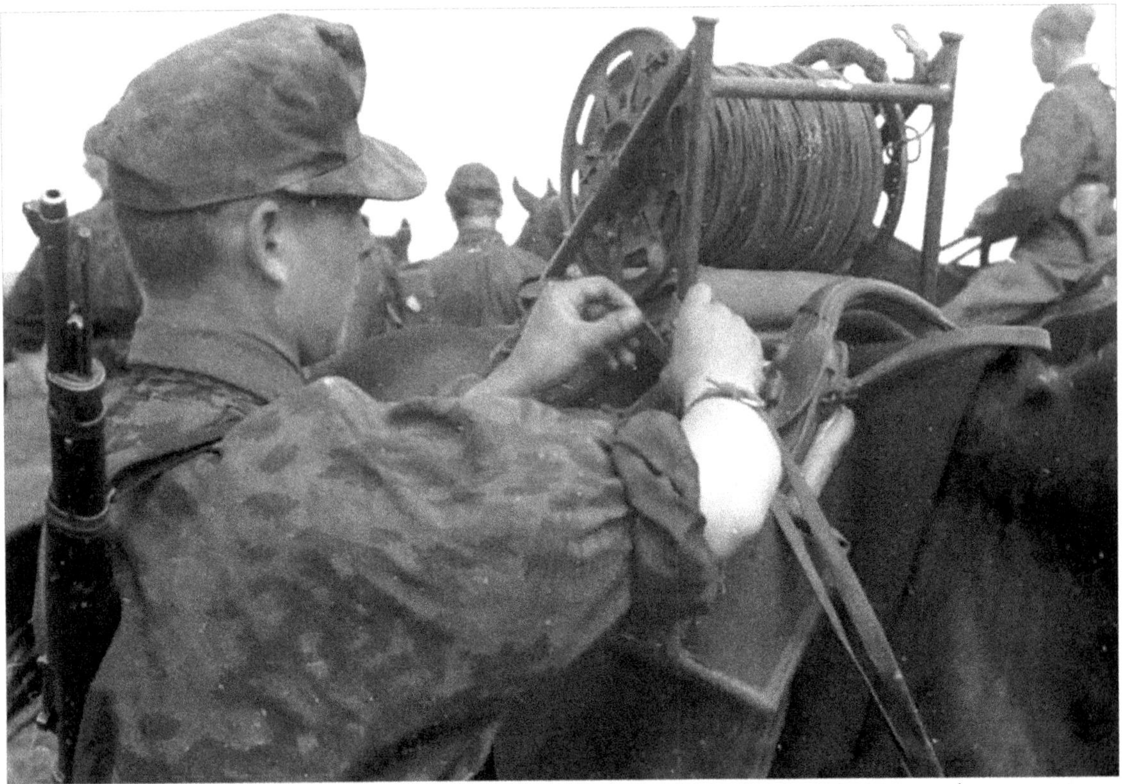

▲ ▼ The following photos (p. 52 to p. 59) by war correspondent Ferdinand Fritsch show a Florian Geyer liaison unit intent on laying telephone cables in the rear. (NARA US Gov.)

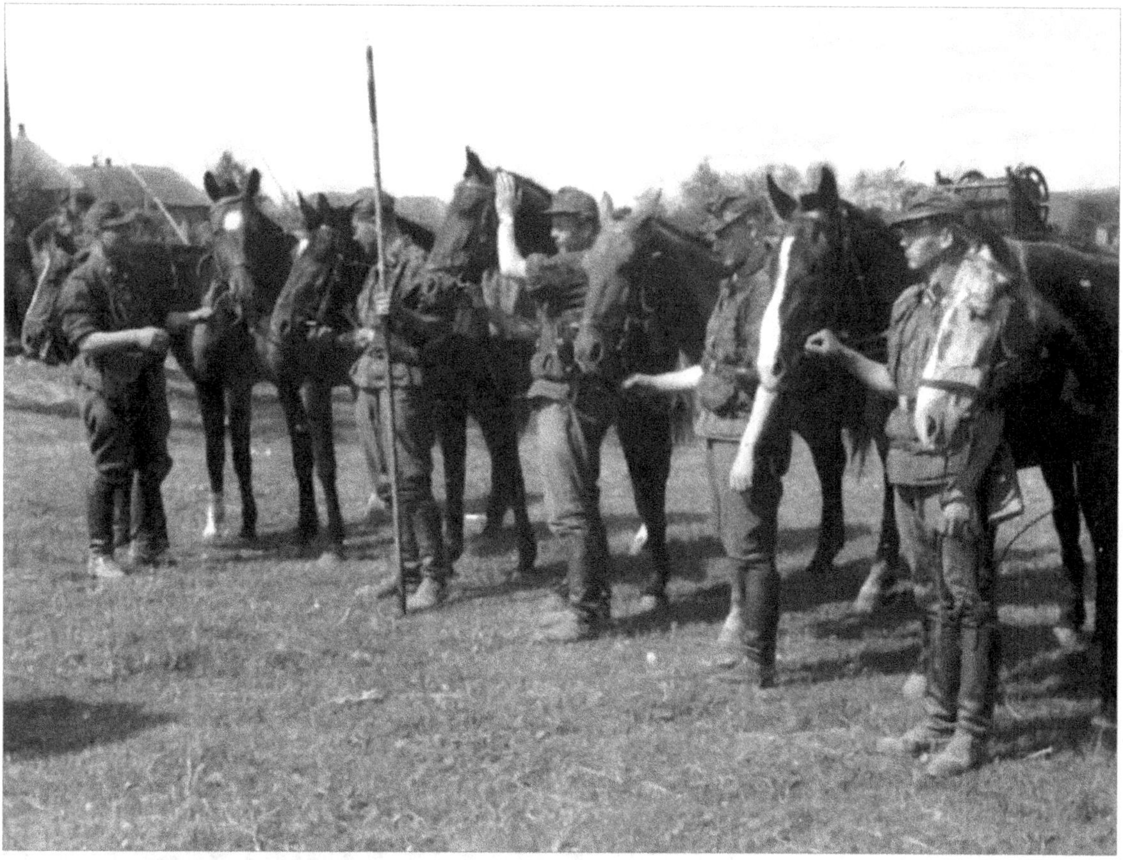

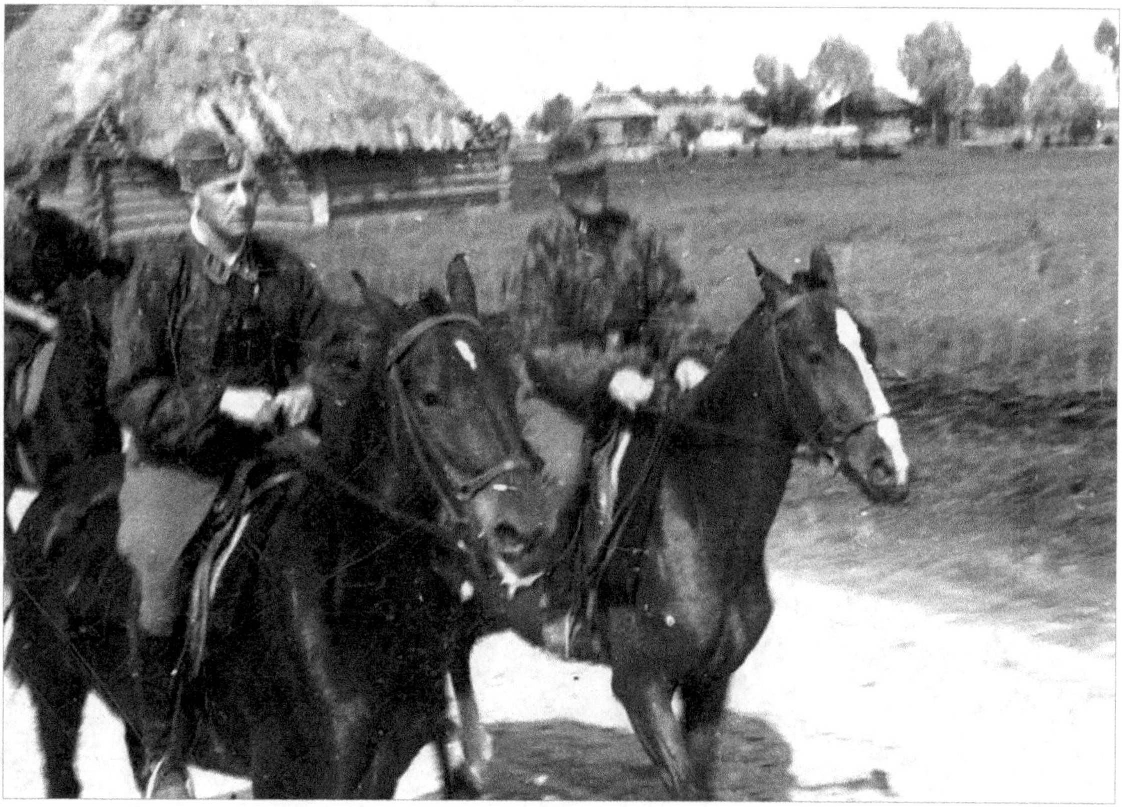

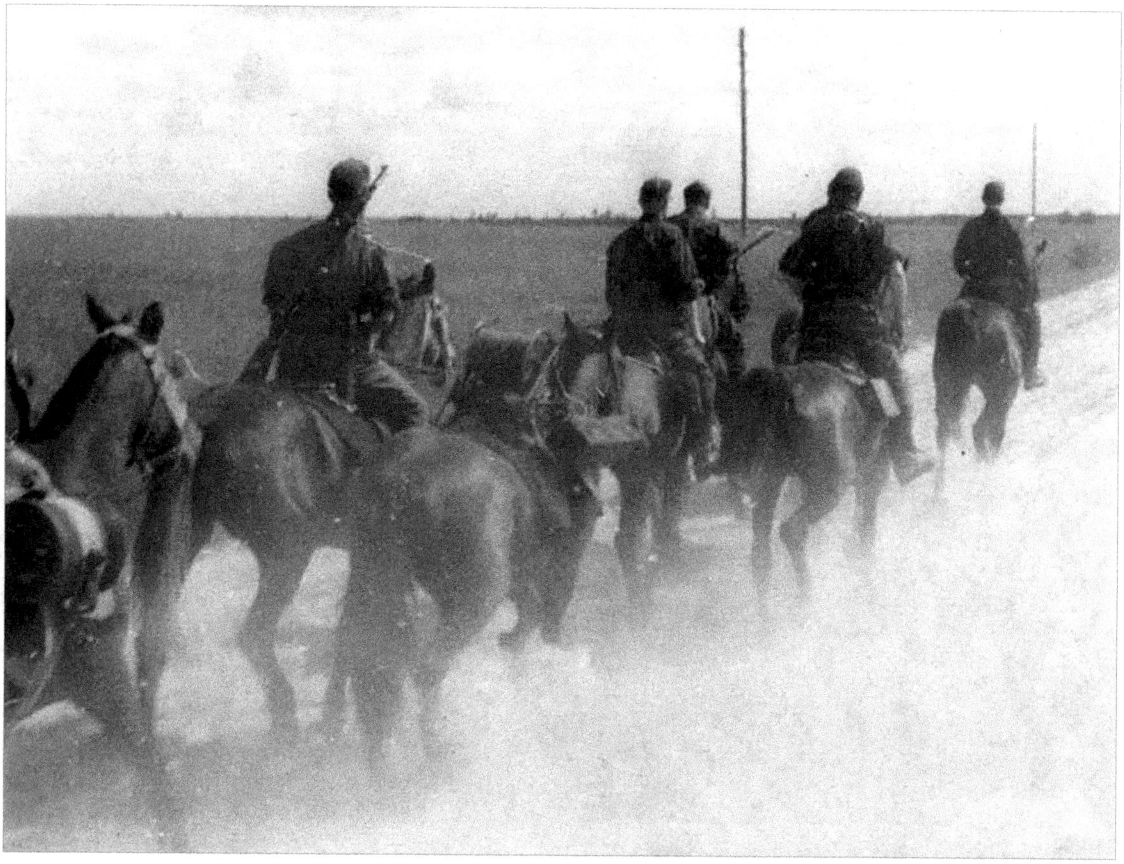

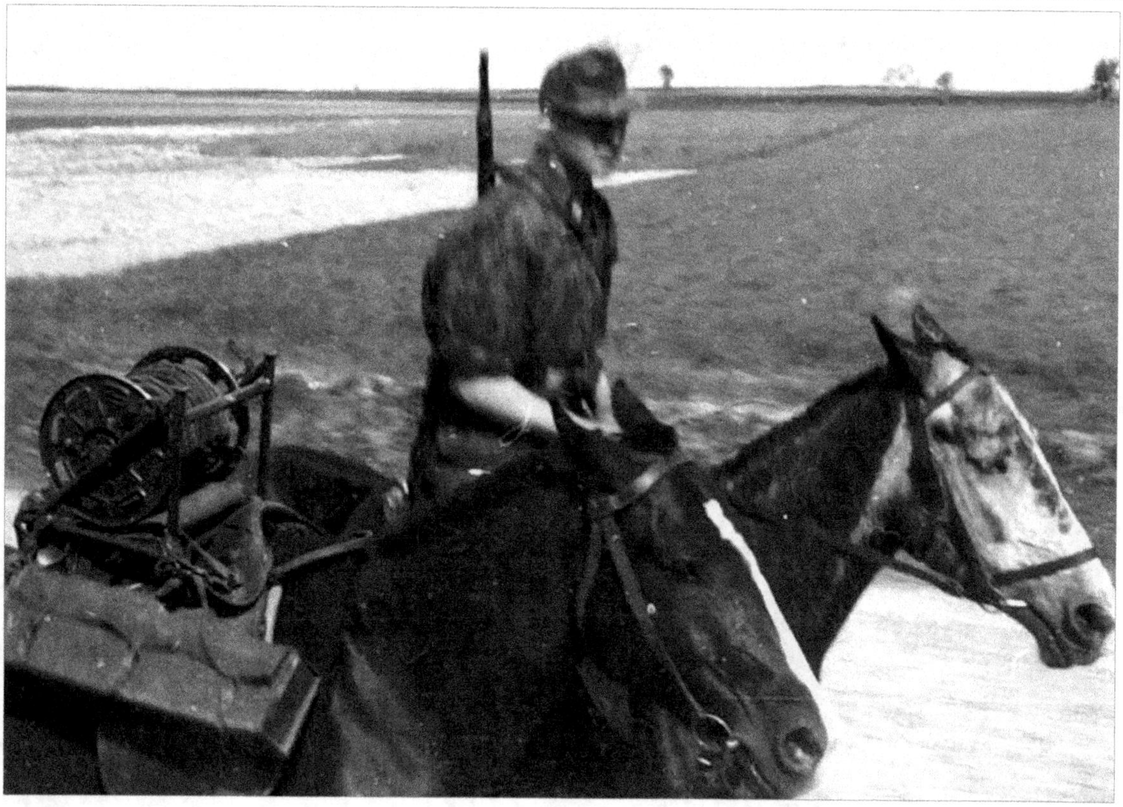

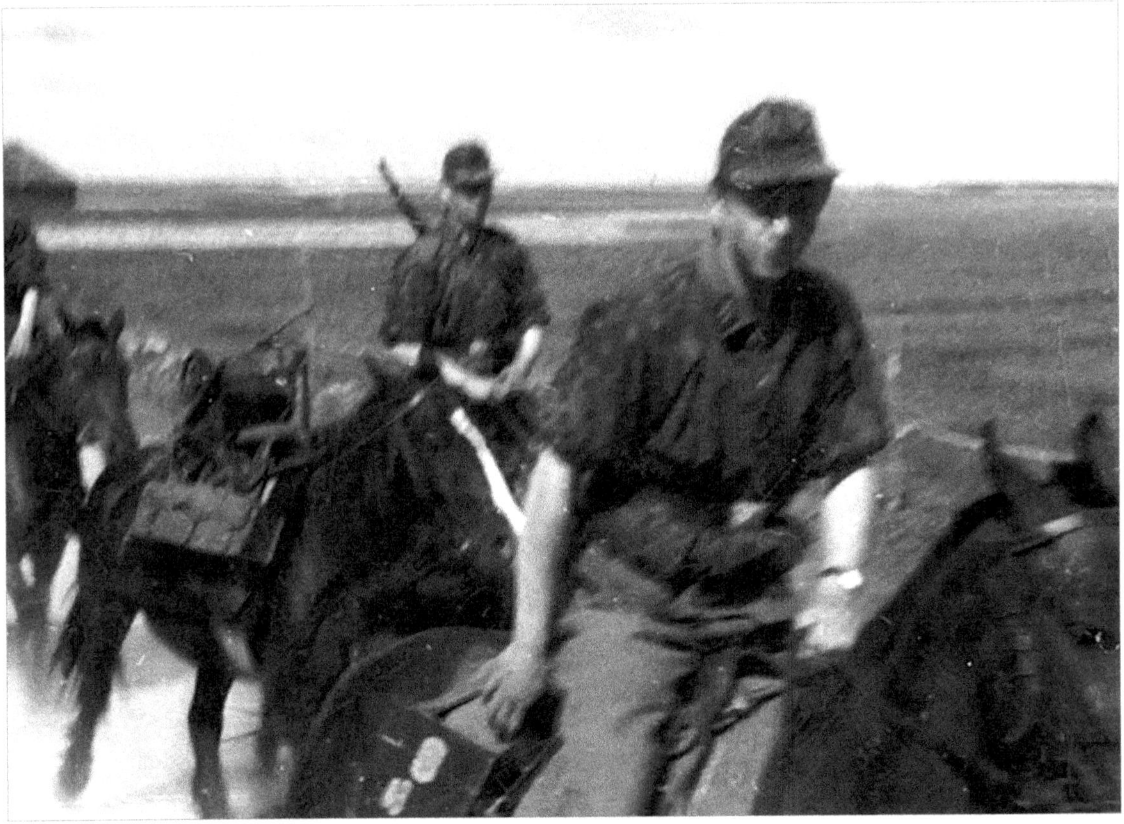

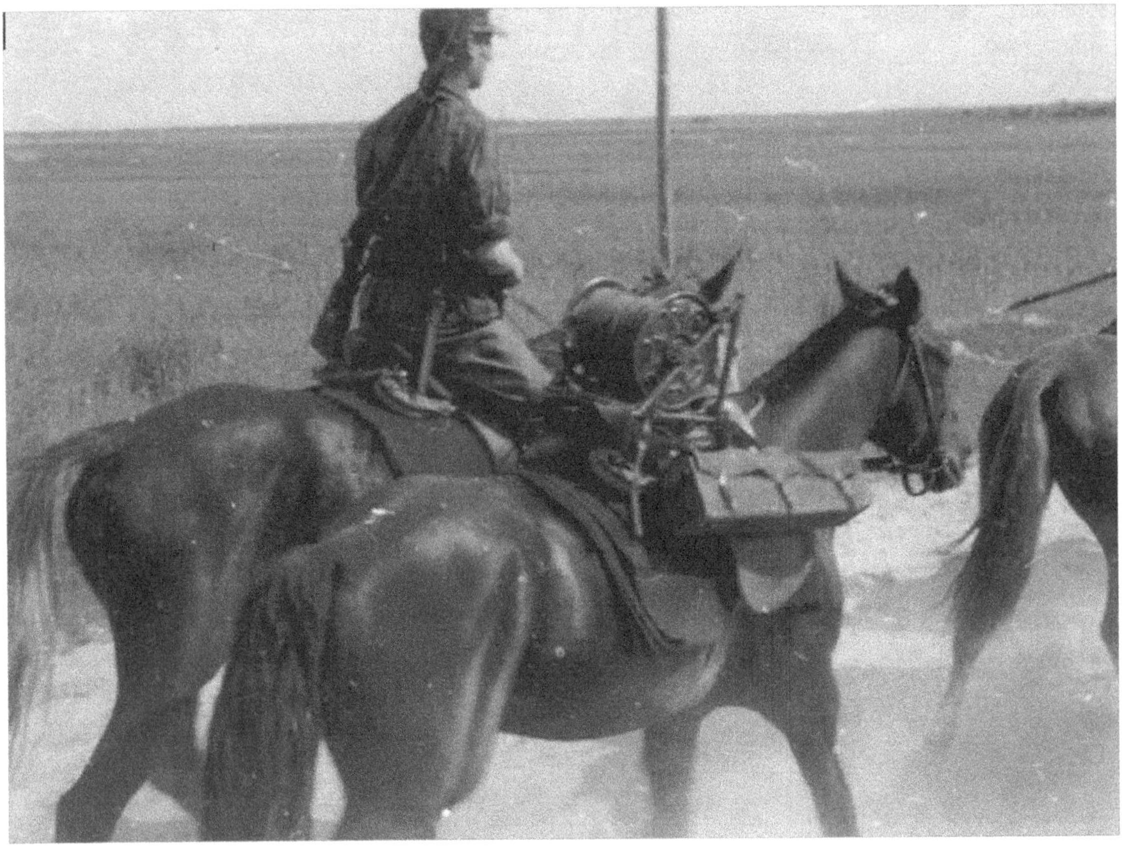

▲ Florian Geyer soldier during a train transfer.

▲ ▼ Pictures of the tank fighter battalion (Abteilung 8) from page 61 to page 65, equipped with StuG IIIs in action in Russia.

▲ ▼ Cavalrymen and tank men of Abteilung 8 during a break in the fighting.

▲ Easter 1944. The local population offers eggs to the SS soldiers.
▼ Close-up of a tank driver from Abteilung 8.

▲ StuG III assault tank alongside a cavalry column. Ancient and modern compared.

THE FIGHTING IN HUNGARY

Meanwhile in Croatia, the division's ranks were being refreshed by new *Volkdeutschland* recruits, most of them between the ages of 17 and 18 and increasingly conscripted by the German administration. The training of these new recruits was occasionally supplemented with real anti-guerrilla operations to counter local partisans.

Equipment was improved, however, with the adoption of the amphibious off-road *schwimmwagens*, and, the artillery regiment was assigned a new battalion numbered as the 2nd, while the 3rd battalion was provided with self-propelled guns: 4 Hummel (Sd.Kfz. 165 with a 150 mm howitzer) and 8 Wespe (Sd.Kfz.124 equipped with a 105 mm howitzer).

On March 12, the SS cavalry division was assigned the name of Florian Geyer belonging to a valiant horseman who played a leading role in the peasant war of 1524 - 1525 and who distinguished himself especially in commanding the peasant faction known as the "Army of Light."

The same month, elements of the division, went to form the Streckenbach *kampfgruppe* engaged in the fight against partisans with in Operation "Cannae" along the Danube.

On April 1, Florian Geyer's command was given to Obersturmbannführer Joachim Rumohr, formerly commander of the same division's artillery regiment, added Oak Leaves to his Knight's Cross for his command actions during the Battle of Budapest.

The division meanwhile was growing stronger. By July its strength reached 12,895 personnel, including 258 officers and 1538 non-commissioned officers.

In August 1944 the great Russian offensive was triggered that wiped out Army Group Center, following this offensive, in the middle of the month, Bessarabia (now Moldavia) was also involved. The German command found itself in serious difficulty, this was also due to the change of front from Romania, which had become an enemy from an ally. At that point all the reserves of Army Group South were kept busy to keep a corridor open in Transylvania so that German troops could withdraw from Romania so as to reform a front along the Carpathians.

The Florian Geyer was engaged along the Mures River beginning in September. There a series of high ground on essentially flat terrain aided defense against attacks by the Soviet VI Guard Army. The reconnaissance battalion sustained fierce fighting in the area between Lichinta and Moresi, forcing the Russians to halt their offensive thrust until pressure from their artillery forced the SS to withdraw on September 17.

As of day 29, the cavalry division, was placed under the XXIX Army Corps, in turn subordinate to the Hungarian II Army, itself part, along with the German VIII Army, of the Wöhler Army Group. To avoid the risks of possible encirclement a retreat from the Carpathians was ordered, again covered by the Florian Geyer with the usual rearguard skirmishes. Thus the line on the Mures River was finally abandoned to the new defensive line called Margarethe east of the Hungarian capital. Thus began the battle for Budapest.

Meanwhile, the situation in Hungary was turning for the worst for the German arms. The Hungarian government of Admiral Horthy was in fact trying to get out of the war, thus abandoning the Germanic ally. Hitler, in order to prevent this situation, decided to implement Operation Panzerfaust, by which he put to the Hungarian government the Arrow Crosses favorable to him and willing to continue the war on his side.

This operation was carried out mainly by SS paratroopers led by Otto Skorzeny on Oct. 15, while the 22nd Maria Theresia Cavalry Division proceeded to occupy vital sectors of the city.

Meanwhile, the Florian Geyer found itself engaged along the Margarethe, in the Tisza River area where a bridgehead had been created, to repel Soviet attacks. On October 29, the Russians, launched a major offensive, convinced they would take the Hungarian capital by the 7th of the same month, but were stopped in front of the Ocsa citadel. On Nov. 4, the Florian Geyer together with elements of the Feldhernhalle Division, which was positioned on the SS left flank, recaptured the towns of Vecses and Ullo. On the right of the Florian Geyer deployed in those same days was the Maria Theresia, all now part of the 3rd *Panzer-Korp*.

On Nov. 6, the SS cavalry launched a series of limited counter-offensives with the aim of capturing some trenches, this led to violent hand-to-hand fighting inside the trenches before they were wrested from the Russian soldiers. The fighting for the occupation of these important trenches, which were essential for maintaining the bridgehead, lasted until the 9th of the same month in which the 22nd Cavalry Division was particularly busy.

On Nov. 15, the 15th Cavalry Regiment, together with the reconnaissance battalion flanked by elements of the Feldhernhalle Division and 12th Reserves Division, recaptured Vecses, lost just days earlier after a bloody battle. In the same days units of the 22nd SS Division were sent to Csepel Island south of Budapest, which was threatened by the Russians.

On November 25, the Russians launched another offensive on Vecses with as many as 35 rifle divisions and 7 mechanized corps from the 2nd Ukrainian Front. Florian Geyer's 8th Reconnaissance Battalion along with armored units of the Feldhernhalle Division launched a counterattack, and the next day the Soviets were again pushed back from Vecses toward Ullo. On November 20, Russian units broke the front between the 22nd SS Division and the 1st Hungarian Hussar Division. Only the next day, with units of German police and the 13th SS Handschar Division, were the Germans able to block the enemy infiltration.

The next few days were of relative calm, the Russians also had to reorganize, and the only notable fighting occurred on Csepel Island.

▲ SS Kavallerie-Division soldier in Hungary in October 1944.

▲ SS scans with binoculars for possible threats.

THE SIEGE OF BUDAPEST AND THE ANNIHILATION OF THE DIVISION

The situation on the German front deteriorated in early December when the Russians managed to break through along the Margarethe Line south and north of the positions held by the SS. In addition, the Soviets, managed to establish bridgeheads on the Danube north of Budapest and south along Lake Balaton, threatening to close the Hungarian capital in a pincer. The German and their allied forces had no more reserves to launch a counterattack and merely defended their positions.
On Dec. 13, the IX *Waffen Gebirgs Korp der SS under the* command of SS-Gruppenführer Karl von Pfeffer-Wildenbruch was put in charge of the defense of Budapest.
On Christmas Day 1944 the grip of the Soviet pincer closed around the Hungarian city.
The 8th SS Cavalry Division meanwhile still held out along the Margarethe, retaining Vecses in its possession, but as the situation around Budapest worsened, it had to send reinforcements inside the city. The 15th regiment was repositioned in Obuda, while the 16th and 18th regiments were placed southwest of Buda with the 8th artillery regiment deployed south of Buda, the move was made on December 26 by falling back from the previous defensive lines along the Margarethe.
Soon the battle turned violent in the city's suburbs as supplies began to run low, especially artillery ammunition. For the besieged, the lack of supplies, was met through the killing of the horses of the two German cavalry divisions trapped in the city, thus managing to feed the defenders, who otherwise would certainly have surrendered their weapons to the enemies.
The Florian Geyer in December alone had 415 killed, 1713 wounded and as many as 381 missing. But the following month was much more challenging for this German cavalry division, as for all units engaged in the harsh siege. Attempts to break the siege by the 4th SS *Panzer-Korp* were all blocked by the Russians, and strict orders not to leave the Hungarian capital marked the final fate of the entire 9th *Waffen Gebirgs Korp* and the Florian Geyer.
The battle was ignited house to house on the low hills of the city suburbs, as in Stalingrad, the battle was dominated by close clashes between infantry due to the difficulty of tanks to intervene on densely built-up terrain. Despite constant artillery and air bombardment, the defenders managed to gain an advantage by taking advantage of the ruins of the now destroyed city.
The defense of the royal castle, where the headquarters and hospital were located, was provided by Obersharführer Friedrich Buck, who, in command of the 5th Squadron of the 18th Regiment and a number of Hungarian soldiers, managed to repel numerous Soviet attacks for several weeks. For these actions he was decorated on January 27 with the Knight's Cross and the gold bar for hand-to-hand combat.
Thus described the fighting in Hungary and the Battle of Budapest by SS-Hauptsturmführer Kurt Portugall, commander of the first battery of SS-Flak-Abt. 8, who, on January 6 itself, had been awarded the important decoration of the German Cross in Gold:

> My battery and I again went into action against tanks in the Bogota area. On September 12, at Lechinta (Maros), of the six Soviet tanks that attacked us, four were destroyed; on September 15 at Ludus (Maros), two more suffered the same fate. On September 25, we were employed with our artillery at Lechinta, so as to provide adequate firepower against the concentration of enemy troops.... Thereafter we withdrew westward.... Budapest. From September 20 to 25, we were detached to the reconnaissance unit of the 8th *Panzerdivision* so as to provide it with artillery support. Telemetry determination was carried out by radio from an SPW (*Schützenpanzerwagen*, armored infantry vehicle) that proceeded side by side with us. The towns of Ajak and Dombradont were recaptured, allowing the surrounded division to break the encirclement. On October 25, together with the same division, we attacked Berkecs north of Nyreghaza.

Thanks to this flank attack, Nyreghaza was recaptured, and the divisional supply train was able to turn back--again, toward a western direction, passing through Hotvan, along the easternmost borders of the Budapest suburbs. On December 24, the First Battery, was positioned on the western bank of the Danube River, near the "Admiral Horthy" bridge, with the guns aiming south. The 2-cm cannon were placed in a firing position in front of the Gellert Hotel. On January 25, the bridge leading to the east bank was blown up and we were completely surrounded in Buda.... The guns were transported back to the university and organized a battle group. *Kampfgruppe* "Portugal" was to cover a gap on Eagle Hill, which had just been abandoned by Hungarian deserters. Here SS-Hauptscharführer Steinberg and SS-Untersturmführer Wilke fell... Violent street-to-street fighting took place in Budapest... from house to house... many casualties[12].

By the end of January, the various units defending Budapest were largely mixed together, as the defensive perimeter gradually shrank. Not even the valor of the elite units could now save the city. On the night of February 11, Pfeffer-Wildenbruch decided to attempt a sortie in the hope that he could save as many men as possible from disaster. The desperate attack was launched with about 24,000 German soldiers plus 20,000 Hungarians, immediately a violent artillery barrage blocked the escape of many of them, only small groups managed to sneak out of the Red Army's grip. For the IX *Waffen Gebirgs Korp* it was the end, only 2 percent made it to safety, while its commander was captured that very night. The Florian Geyer Division followed the fate of the corps to which it belonged by being totally annihilated in an attempt to break through to safety. Most of its men were killed that night as was the division commander Rumohr.

The few survivors of the two cavalry divisions that managed to reach the German lines were framed into a new SS cavalry division the 37th Lützow with which they ended the war.

▲ Panzer Hetzer 38 of the SS Florian Geyer Division in Hungary.

---

12 Ibid, p. 174.

SS-FREIWILLIGEN-KAVALLERIE-DIVISION MARIA THERESIA

As the Russian front came closer to threatening Germany, the Germans went on to create more and more new SS divisions, thus enlisting more and more *Volksdeutsche*, i.e., Germans born outside of Germany, who otherwise could not be framed in Wehrmacht units.

This was the case with the Maria Theresia Division, formed from *Volksdeutsche* of Hungarian origin. It was by an order of the SS-FHA (SS Operational Headquarters), dated April 29, 1944, that a new cavalry division took shape around the nucleus represented by the 17th Cavalry Regiment of the Florian Geyer Division. This division was fresh from the furious fighting that had taken place between March and April of that same year in the Kovel pocket on the Russian front. Here, the cavalry regiment, had faced a severe ordeal away from the rest of the division to which it belonged. Although the regiment emerged victorious from that battle, losses were high and the unit had to be withdrawn from the front for a period of rest and reorganization. The regiment was sent to Kisber in Hungary where, from April, it replenished its ranks to become the core of the future cavalry division.

From this experienced unit, numerous *Volksdeutsche* conscripts were enlisted. Not all of the recruits were, however, unfamiliar with the art of war. Many came from Honved, the Hungarian Army, which, thanks to an agreement between the Germans and Hungarian Regent Horty, were left available for the new SS formation.

The task of organizing the new division was entrusted directly by the SS-FHA to SS-Obergruppenführer Georg Keppler, who, from May 1 to October 30, 1944, was engaged in the establishment of this new unit. Training was carried out in the Kisber, Gyor, and Budapest encampments, while mounted artillery was established in the towns of Bicske, Zsamek, and Raty. The heavy armament and vehicles were mostly of Hungarian origin, while, the SS-FHA, undertook to supply the mounts by requisitioning them in Hungary.

It was originally determined that the division was to comprise as many as four cavalry regiments, numbered from *Freiwilligen-Kavallerie Regiment der SS* 52 up to number 55, with the addition of an artillery regiment, identified as number 22. In reality, the 55th regiment was never formed, while the *Freiwilligen-Kavallerie Regiment der SS* 53 was not formed until October in the Kisber-Boboina sector. The 17th Cavalry Regiment was supposed to assume the number 54 but retained its old numbering.

The new division took the name *SS-Division Ungarn*, but this lasted only from July to mid-September when it was renamed 22nd *SS-Freiwilligen-Kavallerie-Division*. At the end of the year it was officially given the name Maria Theresia, in honor of the great Empress of Austria. The cornflower, considered to be the Empress' favorite flower, was chosen as the unit's emblem; this symbol was used on the right side of the uniform collar.

The division's organizational chart was as follows:

- Divisionsstab
- Freiwilligen-Kavallerie Regiment der SS 52
- Freiwilligen-Kavallerie Regiment der SS 53
- Freiwilligen-Kavallerie Regiment der SS 54 (retained its original designation of 17)
- Freiwilligen-Artillerie Regiment 22
- Panzerjager-Abteilung 22
- Flack-Abteilung 22

Command of the division was assumed in August by SS-Brigadeführer August Zehender, who had previously commanded the *Das-Reich* motorcycle battalion and later the 2nd Cavalry Regiment. Zehender was a very experienced officer, decorated with the Knight's Cross and would lead the division to its tragic end in the Battle of Budapest.

▼ Maria Theresia Division Coat of Arms.

▲ Soldier of the Maria Theresia Division in which the cornflower symbol is prominently displayed.

EARLY DEPLOYMENTS TO THE FRONT

In August, the 17th and 52nd regiments, along with the artillery regiment, were declared combat-ready, this despite the lack of supplies and materials that had burdened the wards of the new division from the beginning.

These first units of the 22nd Division received their baptism of fire in the rear-guard fighting that took place in September at Debreczen in Romania. Later, towards the end of the same month, the 52nd regiment was organized as *Kampfgruppe*, named "*Kampfgruppe* Ameiser" after its commander, SS-Hauptsturmführer Toni Ameiser. Originally the *Kampfgruppe* was led by the 52nd regiment's commander, SS-Sturmbannführer Harry Wiedemann, but he was killed in the early stages of the battle.

On September 30, this unit was sent to the Arad area in Romania with the task of reinforcing the Hungarian front along the Szeged-Arad-Oradea line. The *Kampfgruppe* placed between the 4th and 9th Hungarian Infantry Divisions created a defensive circle around the town of Arad.

On October 1, the Russians, attacked Arad. At first the Soviets launched almost suicidal frontal attacks that, despite the valor of the Russian soldiers, led to nothing but heavy losses in their ranks. Later the Russians changed tactics by attacking the less solid Hungarian units to the north and south of the *Kampfgruppe*. Thus, the Germans, found themselves threatened along the flanks and on October 6 the *Kampfgruppe* was surrounded.

Despite this, the *Kampfgruppe* held their positions until Amaiser decided to take his men out of the pocket, where they were about to be annihilated. To regain their lines to the west, the Germans would have had to cross the Harmas River, but the only bridge still standing was firmly occupied by the Russians, who would have prevented them from crossing it. On October 8, the Soviets, in a violent attack split the *Kampfgruppe in* two; on the southern side came most of the men of the 52nd regiment under the command of SS-Hauptsturmführer Vandieken, who managed to get them to safety by swimming across the Harmas River with horses. Differently went Amaiser and the rest of the men of the *Kampfgruppe, who, in* order to escape the grip of the sack, were forced to take a long route through enemy territory, hiding by day and moving by night. He reached the German lines on October 30 with only 47 survivors, after a journey of two hundred kilometers behind the enemy lines. For his behavior in these events Amaiser was awarded the Knight's Cross on November 1.

Meanwhile, the remainder of the division, was being engaged in the city of Budapest in the important Operation Panzerfaust, which involved restoring the alliance between the Hungarians and the Germans, after Admiral Horthy had entered into negotiations with the Allies for a change of alliances. When Hungarian Regent Horthy radioed on October 15 that negotiations with the Soviets had begun, Operation Panzerfaust was initiated.

The conduct of this operation saw the 22nd Division engaged as support to the main force led by Otto Skorzeny and his paratroopers. The intervention of the cavalry was in every way decisive in occupying all the focal points of the Hungarian capital, including the government palace, thus preventing the Honved from any attempt to react, this allowed the Germans to carry out the coup with minimal bloodshed. In the operation there were, in fact, only four deaths among the Germans and three among the Hungarians, all of whom fell in the clash that took place over possession of the city's castle.

▲ An SS during the clashes in Hungary.

▲ Light cavalry of the SS-freiwilligen-kavallerie-division Maria Theresia.

▼ Soldier of the Maria Theresia Division at the conclusion of the coup in Budapest.

THE BATTLE OF BUDAPEST

The success of Operation Panzerfaust was short-lived for the soldiers of Maria Theresia. The approach of the Soviet army to the Hungarian capital in early November necessitated the deployment of the entire division for its defense along the defensive line known as Margarethe.

The sector assigned to the cavalry of the 22nd Division was located southeast of Budapest, forming a defensive ring between Dunaharztil and Taksony, with the 8th SS Cavalry Division on its left flank and the Danube on its right side. German units in this sector were assigned to the 3rd *Panzer-Korps*. As early as November 5, the cavalrymen were engaged in a violent enemy offensive in the Karola area. The next day the SS launched a counteroffensive to regain lost ground and relieve Russian pressure on their Florian Geyer comrades who were fighting hard in the area around Vecses, a key point of the German defense. That day, Zehender's soldiers, managed to capture some enemy trenches in furious hand-to-hand combat that resulted in heavy losses to both contenders.

The 22nd Division was engaged in hard fighting until the end of November. Attacks and counterattacks followed each other in a frantic and disorderly manner. In particular, the Budapest-Ocsa railway was attacked by the Russians on the ninth day, forcing the SS to retreat two kilometers along the railway line itself. It was not until the next day that a counteroffensive east of Soroksar succeeded in recovering a few hundred meters, which were then abandoned to the enemy because of the crisis that had affected the other divisions of III *Panzer-Korps*.

On November 11 Zehender's division succeeded in closing a dangerous one-kilometer-wide gap that had opened northwest of a railroad bridge in the vicinity of the town of Gyal. This last counterattack was particularly bloody, and the divisions engaged in the fighting soon found themselves short of men.

On the 15th, the Soviets, attacked the island of Csepel on the Danube east of Szigetszentmiclas, forcing Zehender to detach a *Kampfgruppe* from his 1,000-strong division there in order to establish a new front line. The attack on the island was supported by a mechanized infantry battalion from the Feldhernhalle Division and a battalion of Hungarian volunteers. The operation was successful in driving the Russians off the island, thanks in part to the latter's lack of heavy weapons.

On the 18th the Russians unleashed a new offensive in the III *Panzer-Korps* sector, strong with 35 rifle divisions and 7 mechanized corps from the II Ukrainian Front.

Repulsed once again at Vecses, the Russians attacked on the 20th along the junction between the 22nd SS Division and the 1st Hungarian Hussar Division, managing to break through and reach the suburbs of Budapest. The intervention of the 13th SS Handschar Division the next day succeeded in restoring the front line.

The following days were employed by the contenders to reorganize for future offensives. After these battles, the division had lost, as of May, 1503 men dead, wounded and missing, while, the total force, remained at 8,000.

In the days between December 4 and 6 a number of Russian patrols sent to scout along the Ocsa-Kispest railway line were repulsed. While, from the 11th of the same month, the only clashes with the Soviets took place on the island of Csepel, where the 22nd Division took over the 1st Armored Division of the Honved to its dependencies. On Dec. 13, the 9th *Waffen Gebirgs Korp der SS, under the* command of SS-Gruppenführer Karl von Pfeffer-Wildenbruch, was put in charge of the defense of Budapest.

From the 22nd Russian offensive actions increased sharply. Finally, on Christmas Day, Budapest was surrounded by 250,000 Soviet troops, and on the 27th Vesces finally fell to the Russians. From the next day the first difficulties in supplying the troops inside the pocket began to be felt. In that month of December alone the 22nd Division had lost about 1,000 men, including fallen, wounded and missing. Equally high were the losses among the other forces engaged in this battle, in particular many were Hungarian deserters, especially among the 10th and 12th infantry divisions.

On Dec. 26, only two days into the siege, some units of the Maria Theresia, posted in the west in the city of Budapest, managed to escape from the besieged city and place themselves safely within their own lines. These were mostly members of the logistical services.

Supply difficulties within the pocket were solved by means of an airlift, taking advantage of the Hungarian capital's airport runways and building new ones. Thanks to the airlift many wounded could thus be evacuated. On December 27, the loss of Budapest's main airport, located in the eastern sector of the city, forced the Germans to build a new runway in the northern part of Buda, taking advantage of a city park called Vémezo.

The problem of food supplies was, however, partly solved by the 30,000 horses belonging to the two cavalry divisions, which, stuck inside the city, served to feed the besieged.

The 22nd Division, despite heavy losses, was forced to increase the width of its front, which had to extend to the entire southern part of Budapest, reaching as far as Budaros, passing through Csepel Island.

The fighting continued to unfold furiously house to house. On January 6, a counteroffensive carried out by the 22nd Division along the hills south of the capital led to the annihilation of an entire Soviet regiment after a particularly bitter battle.

As attempts by the 4th SS *Panzer-Korps to* break the siege failed, the besieged city's defensive perimeter shrank further and further. On Jan. 17, the last Axis troops were evacuated from Pest and the Franz-Joseph Bridge connecting the western and eastern parts was destroyed.

On January 19, the remnants of the Maria Theresia Division were hard at work recapturing the airfield located in the western sector of the city. By the same day, however, the size of the pocket had shrunk to a square 1 km long by 1 km deep. In this situation any airlift was doomed to failure. Wards were fighting for survival now mixed together.

▲ Soldiers of Maria Theresia in Budapest.

By the end of January, the situation was hopeless. Food rations had dwindled at this point, and the only drinkable water was snow that was melted in gavels. Ammunition was also beginning to run low, and supplies could only be parachuted in.

The commander of the besieged Pfeffer-Wildenbruch did not, however, want to accept an unconditional surrender as happened at Stalingrad; he decided instead to attempt a desperate, albeit belated, sortie. The attack was to take place in two directions to the west. The 8th Florian Geyer Division and 13th *Panzerdivision* would lead the main attack, while the 22nd Maria Theresia Division would follow on the right flank, covering the flank and rear of the first two units.

On the night of Feb. 11, the Germans and their allies divided into small groups tried to break through the enemy lines as had been established, but, the enemy reaction, was violent. A furious artillery barrage blocked any organized attempt in crossing the enemy lines.

This attempt failed and marked the end of all the units engaged in the defense of Budapest; out of 24,000 German soldiers only 785 managed to gain their lines.

The Maria Theresia Division ceased to exist that very night. Brigadeführer August Zehender fell fighting along with many of his officers; the commander of the antiaircraft battalion, SS-Hauptsturmführer Weckmann, preferred suicide rather than fall into enemy hands. Of the two SS cavalry divisions, only 170 men managed to save themselves.

Only the 52nd Maria Theresia Regiment, a veteran of the Arad sack, was partially spared from annihilation. In the following months from this unit took shape the SS-Kavallerie *Regiment* 94 of the new SS Lützow Cavalry Division, which, regrouping the survivors of the two cavalry divisions returning from Budapest, would fight in the final stages of the war.

▲ The Knight's Cross Obersturmbannführer der Reserve Anton Ameiser in command of the SS-Freiwilligen-Kavallerie 94 regiment.

THE 37TH SS-FREIWILLIGEN-KAVALLERIE-DIVISION LUTZOW

The destruction of the 9th *Waffen Gebirgs Korp der SS* was a disaster for the German forces, however, in order to maintain the tradition of a cavalry corps, a new cavalry unit was created with the surviving cavalrymen from the divisions destroyed in Budapest that would be joined by some adolescent *volksdeutsche* conscripts of Hungarian origin. This was the 37th *SS-Freiwilligen-Kavallerie-Division Lützow*, named in honor of Ludwig Adolf Wilhelm von Lützow (1782 - 1834) cavalry commander during the Napoleonic Wars.

In January 1945, the core of the new unit, was assembled near Bratislava under the leadership of SS-Oberführer Waldemar Fegelein replaced in March by SS-Standartenführer Karl Gesele. The future division included as many as three cavalry regiments, each based on two battalions. The units were assembled at the various training and reinforcement camps of the Maria Theresia Division and then assembled in March at Marchfeld, along the Hungarian-Slovak border, presenting the following organizational chart:

- SS-Kavallerie Regiment 92
- SS-Kavallerie Regiment 93
- SS-Kavallerie Regiment 94
- SS-Artillerie-Abteilung 37 (two batteries of FH18 10.5 cm)
- SS-Aufklärungs-Abteilung 37
- SS-Panzerjäger-Abteilung 37 (a company equipped with Hetzer)
- SS-Pionier-Bataillon 37
- SS-Nachrichten-Kompanie 37
- SS-Sanitäts-Abteilung 37
- SS-Nachschub-Truppen 37
- Feldersatz-Bataillon 37

The lack of men and weapons made it very difficult to reach the division's planned full strength. In addition, the situation at the front was becoming increasingly dramatic and required the immediate deployment of every combat-ready unit. As early as the end of March, a *Kampfgruppe* was created from the division, led by SS-Oberstrumbannführer Karl-Heinz Keitel (son of the more famous Field Marshal Wilhelm Keitel), for this reason named *SS-Kampfgruppe* Keitel, aggregated with the First SS *Panzerkorps in* turn belonging to what remained of the 6th SS Panzer Army engaged in covering the retreat from Hungary to Austria.

The 92nd Regiment was deployed intensively along the Austrian borders from the beginning of April, suffering heavy losses partly due to the inexperience of its soldiers but managing to achieve local successes, repelling an attack on the town of Neuhof with the rest of the division holding on to the Aspern - Stadlau - Hirschstetten line but, when the Soviets crossed the Danube on April 12, the division, had to retreat to a more westerly defensive line.

In early May, Keitel, ordered the 6th SS Panzer Army to make contact with American forces advancing from the west to negotiate a surrender, which happened on May 7 when an American delegation was met. The negotiations ended on May 10 with the surrender of German forces and the destruction of armaments. The 37th Division still had two Hetzer tanks left, which were destroyed. In the following days, the soldiers of the 37th, surrendered to the Americans as they came from the east, at random, ending up in American captivity.

The testimony of the commander of the 8th Squadron belonging to *SS-Kavallerie Regiment* 93 about the last stages of the war is interesting and worth reporting:

> On April 1, we rode through Vienna during an air raid, and settled for the night in the Oberlaa district along the Reichsbrücke. The other three squadrons (the 5th, 6th and 7th), which had left as soon as we got on the train, had to descend along the road and disappeared before my eyes. We retreated south again, staying in contact with the enemy until Pottenstein, where we emptied a depot containing foodstuffs and clothing. With the Russians breathing down our necks, we continued toward Klausenleopoldsdorf. We entrenched ourselves at Schöpflgitter, above a road junction in the forest; on our right were elements of the 12th *SS-Panzerdivision*, on the left, the Leibstandarte. There was a high number of casualties at that location. Our headquarters were in Obergröd, and later in Forsthof. The fighting moved behind Schöpflgitter where some Russians had been captured and threw some hand grenades at us. That night we stayed in reserve and rested in a barn and then moved from Schöpflgitter to Kaumberg. There, some of us, lost contact with the rest of our troops. We could hear the sounds of battle all around us using them to find our way back. When we reached the Klaumhöhe - Untertriesting road, we found some Soviet soldiers from the towed wagon units resting having a bite to eat after stacking their weapons in pyramids right in the middle of the road, as if they were in peacetime. Immediately we came out of the forest shouting "Hooray," crossing the road totally unharmed so that we were reunited with the rest of our unit in the cemetery northwest of Kaumberg. Kaumberg had already been occupied by the enemy. Two days later I attempted to recapture Kaumberg with artillery support, which was also to cover a simultaneous attack by another Wehrmacht unit. This support never materialized and, without any heavy weapons with us, we failed. The headquarters was placed in Araburg. We were pressed toward Heinfeld, with the Soviets moving down the valley and us in the mountains. There we found some Soviets around the marketplace in a fire truck, blowing their horns and bells. Unexpectedly, we were taken over by Wehrmacht units and joined *Kampfgruppe* "Keitel" in a motorized convoy down the Pax valley, via Kleinzell, Hölle, Kalte Kuchl and Jagerwirt. The Second of the 93rd Regiment was using the Hutbauer Inn as a command post. There, we took position on a knoll with our cannons transported from Gutenstein. There was even an anti-tank gun that we positioned at the top of the hill. We had to work hard given the presence of snow everywhere. After a few days, I was transferred to our neighbors to our left, a Wehrmacht unit whose colonel had been hospitalized. The Russians deliberately attacked us every night after they had guzzled a large amount of alcohol, only to be wiped out each night with grenades, a couple of Panzerfausts and stone blocks. Darkness was also on our side; men from Skorzeny-dressed in civilian clothes or wearing Russian uniforms-went through our position using code names. From Streimling, I could see the road intersection of Urgerbach and Perlgraben and watch the comings and goings of enemy supplies. Once we took aim with our guns, we were able to destroy them substantially with the bazookas we had requested.
>
> On the afternoon of May 8, after a brief meeting at battalion headquarters, our unit was taken over the same night; we had been instructed to use every precaution and take away all our weapons and equipment. We had not been told that the war was over, only that we were to head for Mariazel, which we reached on the morning of May 9. It was there, during a break, that we heard that the war was over and that agreements had been reached with the Americans, to whom we surrendered, ending up as prisoners in Altenmarkt on May 10 after crossing the Enns River...[13]

The Lützow Division ended its existence that same May 10, along with the majority of the German army. Other cavalry units, such as Florian Geyer's replacement company and cavalry cadets from the Weende school near Göttingen, ended up being sent to Prague where they disappeared during the final fighting against the Soviets around this city at the end of the war.

---

13 Ibid, p. 183.

▲ Soldiers from Lützow move quickly on horseback.

▼ Lützow Division Coat of Arms.

CONCLUSIONS

The Florian Geyer division had started as a unit prepared to fight partisan forces but also found itself performing front-line tasks for which it was not prepared; as the war and contingent needs continued, the latter task predominated over guerrilla fighting. Compared to the other SS divisions the Florian Geyer found itself at a disadvantage in regular combat especially with regard to the tactical preparation of the middle officers whose mistakes caused many losses in the division's ranks. These shortcomings were made up, in part, by the strong esprit de corps of the division's men, which never failed even at the end, when its ranks included, for the most part, *Volksdeutsche* conscripts, thus making it an elite unit.

The fortunes of the 22nd Maria Theresia Division remain closely linked to the terrible Battle of Budapest. This SS unit was able to hold its own against the preponderant enemy forces, this despite the fact that the division's formation was only a few months before the decisive battle. Most of its men were conscripts, moreover, its armament, was certainly not of the most advanced. Nevertheless, its soldiers preferred total annihilation rather than surrender, demonstrating uncommon valor.

Although the two cavalry divisions had recognized fewer Knight's Crosses than the main SS divisions (the Leibstandarte had 58 and Das Reich 69), they still had a number of Knight's Crosses, despite the fact that their employment was mainly related to anti-guerrilla duties, away from the major offensives on the Eastern Front and the small number of soldiers employed by the cavalry. The Florian Geyer had as many as 22 Knight's Crosses and, the Maria Theresia, in the short time of her existence, received 6 Knight's Crosses, all decorations awarded to her soldiers.

The experience gained in the more congenial task of anti-guerrilla warfare demonstrated the effectiveness of mounted units in difficult terrain. Although the last fighting between mounted troops on the front lines occurred only in the early period of the war, making the cavalry weapon now obsolete in a modern conflict, its activity was well appreciated in the fight against partisans, so much so that, still in the 1970s, mounted units were successfully deployed in the Rhodesian War, which, in the difficult African terrain, made life difficult for guerrilla movements.

▲ Fegelein and Himmler confabulate followed by the SS chief's staff (Bundesarchiv).

▲ German prisoners including SS elements.

▼ Rhodesian cavalry in search of guerrillas in the African bush.

▲ Waffen SS Cavalry Brigade, 23 September 1941 Russia (Bundesarchiv).

▼ Mounted SS elements uncover a clandestine arms cache in Russia (Afiero Archive).

▲ SS cavalry in the occupied Soviet Union, June 1942 (Bundesarchiv).

▲ SS of a cavalry division in a marching pasusa in Russia (Bundesarchiv).

▲ SS officer in camouflage outfit of a cavalry division in Russia (magazine of the time).

▲ SS cavalry division engaged in a rastrektion (Bandenbekämpfung) May 1943.

▼ Trompeterkorps of the 8th SS-Kavallerie-Division 'Florian Geyer'.

HIERARCHY AND COMMANDERS OF SS CAVALRY DIVISIONS

Florian Geyer Division

SS-Brigadeführer Gustav Lombard (March - April 1942)
SS-Gruppenführer Hermann Fegelein (April - August 1942)
SS-Obergruppenführer Wilhelm Bittrich (August 1942 - February 15, 1943)
SS-Brigadeführer Fritz Freitag (15 February 1943 - 20 April 1943)
SS-Brigadeführer Gustav Lombard (April 20, 1943 - May 14, 1943)
SS-Gruppenführer Hermann Fegelein (May 14, 1943-September 13, 1943)
SS-Gruppenführer Bruno Streckenbach (September 13, 1943 - October 22, 1943)
SS-Gruppenführer Hermann Fegelein (October 22, 1943 - January 1, 1944)
SS-Gruppenführer Bruno Streckenbach (January 1, 1944 - April 14, 1944)
SS-Brigadeführer Gustav Lombard (April 14, 1944 - July 1, 1944)
SS-Brigadeführer Joachim Rumohr (from July 1, 1944)

Maria Theresia Division

SS-Brigadeführer August Zehender (April 21, 1944 - February 11, 1945)

Lützow Division

SS-Standartenführer Waldemar Fegelein (February 1945 - March 1945)
SS-Standartenführer Karl Gesele (March 1945 - May 1945)

Hierarchy

Mannschaften   troop and graduates

SS-Bewerber   military trainee
SS-Anwärterallievo   official
SS-Manns   Private
SS-Grenadierschüzeszes soldier simple 2nd class
SS-Oberschüzes soldier   simple 1st class
                                SS-Sturmanncaporale
                                SS-Rottenführercaporalmaggiore

Unterführer   NCOs

                        SS-Unterscharführersergente
SS-Scharführersergent major
                        SS-Oberscharführer Marshal
                        SS-Hauptscharführer-Major Marshal   2nd Class
                        SS-Sturmscharführer-Major Marshal   1st Class

Untere Führer officers   inferior

                                      SS-Untersturmführer second lieutenant
                                      SS-Obersturmführer tenente
                                      SS-Hauptsturmführer Captain

Mittlere Führer   senior officers

                                      SS-Sturmbannführer
SS-Obersturmbannführer tenant Col.

Höhere Führer   general officers

                                      SS-Standartenführer colonel
SS-Oberführer colonel brigadier
                                      SS-Brigadeführer general
SS-Gruppenführer generale of division
SS-Obergruppenführer general of army corps
SS-Oberst-Gruppenführer generale d'armata.
Reichsführer-SS commander-in-chief

▲ SS rider holds the bridle of two beautiful equine specimens. Ferdinand Frick (NARA US Gov.).

▲ Hans Georg Otto Hermann Fegelein, one of the most important figures of the Third Reich. Himmler's dauphin, he married Eva Braun's sister, then became Hitler's brother-in-law for a few hours. He was shot in the Chancellery bunker.

▲ Gustav Lombard, several times commander of the Florian Geyer.

▲ Karl Gesele with Hermann Fegelein. Gesele was the last commander of the Lützow Division.

▲ Joachim Rumohr, another Florian Geyer commander.

▲ Waldemar Fegelein, Hermann's brother. He commanded Florian Geyer's 2nd cavalry regiment.

▲ SS-Brigadeführer August Zehender, former commander of the Maria Theresia Division.

▲ Wilhelm Bittrich, who also commanded the Florian Geyer. On the left Hermann Fegelein.

▲ In the centre of the photo, next to Himmler, is Bruno Streckenbach, twice commander of the Florian Geyer. He was also one of the top Nazi criminals as organiser of the notorious Einsatzgruppen.

BIBLIOGRAPHY

- Charles Trang, *La Division Floian Geyer*, HEIMDAL, 2000.

- Paul J. Wilson, *Himmler's Calvary: The Equestrain SS 1930-45*, Schiffler Military History, 2000.

- Jeffrey T.Fowler, *Axis Cavalry in world war II*, OSPREY.

- Ian Baxter, *8th SS Cavalry Division Florian Geyer: Rare Photographs from Wartime Archives (Images of War)* 2023

- Herman Fegelein, *SS-Kavallerie im Osten: Vom 1. SS-Totenkopf-Reiterregiment zur SS-Reiter-Brigade Fegelein*

- Matteo Simonetti, *Hitler e Fichte - Capire il Nazionalsocialismo*, Nexus Edizioni, Battaglia terme, 2022.

- M.Afiero *The 8th Waffen-SS Cavalry Division "Florian Geyer": An Illustrated History (Divisions of the Waffen-SS, 4)*

- Robin Lumsden, *La vera storia delle SS*, Newton e Compton editori, Roma, 1999.

- G. Williamson, *Storia illustrata delle SS*, Newton e Compton editori, Roma, 2001.

- G. Gigli, *La seconda guerra mondiale*, Lucio Pugliese editore, 1986.

- F. Duprat, *Le campagne militari delle Waffen SS*, Ritter editore, 2010.

- SS-Standartenführer Waldemar Fegelein di Sergio Volpe, rivista Fronti di Guerra n° 85.

- R.Landwher, *Steadfast Hussars The Last Cavalry Div*

- SS volunteers on the Eastern Front original SS book of the Waffen-SS. 1943.

- Pieper, Henning (2015). *Fegelein's Horsemen and Genocidal Warfare: The SS Cavalry Brigade in the Soviet Union*. Houndmills, UK: Palgrave Macmillan.

- Rolf Michaelis *Cavalry Divisions of the Waffen-SS.* 2010.

- Rolf Michaelis *Albert Schwenn's Memories of the Waffen-SS: An SS Cavalry Division Veteran Remembers (Memories of the Waffen-SS, 2)*.

- Helmut Grund, *The Nazi Murder Squad: The Confession of Helmut Grund, Waffen-SS Cavalry.*

- Mark C. Yerger, *Riding East: The SS Cavalry Brigade in Poland and Russia 1939-1942 (Schiffer Military History)* 1997.

Siti visitati:

- SS-Kriegsberichter Archive (kriegsberichter-archive.com)

TITOLI GIÀ PUBBLICATI - TITLES ALREADY PUBLISHING

BOOKS TO COLLECT

www.ingramcontent.com/pod-product-compliance
Lightning Source LLC
LaVergne TN
LVHW081539070526
838199LV00056B/3711